Marvin Richardson Vincent

Gates into the Psalm-country

Marvin Richardson Vincent

Gates into the Psalm-country

ISBN/EAN: 9783744773508

Printed in Europe, USA, Canada, Australia, Japan

Cover: Foto ©Lupo / pixelio.de

More available books at **www.hansebooks.com**

GATES INTO THE PSALM-COUNTRY.

INTO THE

PSALM-COUNTRY.

BY

MARVIN R. VINCENT, D.D.,
PASTOR OF "THE CHURCH OF THE COVENANT," NEW YORK.

"Open to me the gates of righteousness: I will go into them, and I will praise the Lord;
"This gate of the Lord into which the righteous shall enter."
PSALM cxviii.; 19, 20.

NEW YORK:
CHARLES SCRIBNER'S SONS,
743 AND 745 BROADWAY.

COPYRIGHT BY
CHARLES SCRIBNER'S SONS.
1878.

TROW'S
PRINTING & BOOKBINDING CO.,
205-213 East 12th St.,
NEW YORK.

To

MY PEOPLE,

"The Church of the Covenant,"

WHOM IT HAS BEEN MY JOY TO LEAD THROUGH THESE "GATES,"

I Dedicate this Volume.

PREFACE.

THIS volume is not intended as a critical treatise. It is for the closet rather than for the study: for the average Bible-reader rather than for the scholar. The several chapters are, as the title imports, merely "gates," opening here and there into this wonderful Psalm-region, and leading to outlooks from which, it is hoped, readers may catch glimpses of the ineffable beauty and richness of this land of sacred song, and be stimulated to longer journeys and to more minute researches.

Almost all of these chapters were originally given to my own people in the form of lectures or sermons; and while I have in some instances modified, or partially recast them, I have suffered them to retain much of the familiarity and directness of address which mark the spoken discourse as distinguished from the essay.

Some of these studies, it will be observed, deal with entire Psalms, others with single verses. Yet it may be found, in some cases, that the single verse lies in the cleavage-line of the whole Psalm.

I shall be thankful, if, in any degree, I can make others share the feeling which has been constantly present to myself in the preparation of this volume —how habitually the Psalms fall into the track of New Testament thought and sentiment. At a time when so many readers are influenced, unconsciously, perhaps, by the patronizing tone of certain modern critics towards these inspired songs, to regard them mainly as interesting relics, and expressions of a crude morality and of an infantile faith,—it may be of service to show, even in this unsystematic and fragmentary way, how many of them fit into the best and ripest phases of Christian thought, and adapt themselves to the most advanced ideals of Christian duty. If I may use the words of the eloquent Bishop of Derry: "The Psalms are interwoven with the texture of the New Testament. Christianity is responsible for the Psalter with its very life. The golden key of the Psalter lies in a pierced hand. There are many who profess to expel Christ from the Psalms in the interest of the Psalms themselves. But the Psalter as a living thing, and the association with it of our Incarnate Lord, stand together. Those were memorable words which Mr. Coleridge wrote upon the margin of his Prayer Book: 'As a transparency on some night of public rejoicing, seen by common day, with the lamps from within removed, even such would the Psalms be to me, uninterpreted by the Gospel.'"*

In the versions of the Psalms, I have mostly followed Canon Perowne, and in the essay on the Pilgrim Psalms, and in the chapter entitled "The Gate to the Harvest-field," I have to express my great obligation to the charming little volume on the Pilgrim Psalms, by the Rev. Samuel Cox, of Corporation Oaks, Nottingham, the editor of the "Expositor."

COVENANT PARSONAGE, *October* 21, 1878.

---

* "Witness of the Psalms to Christ," by William Alexander, D.D., D.C.L., Bishop of Derry and Raphoe. Bampton Lectures for 1876.

CONTENTS.

	PAGE
I.—THE ORCHARD GATE	3
II.—THE GATE TO THE THRESHING-FLOOR	21
III.—THE ORATORY GATE	39
IV.—THE PASTURE GATE	53
V.—THE REGISTRY GATE	75
VI.—THE TREASURY GATE	91
VII.—THE GATE TO THE CONFESSIONAL	109
VIII.—THE GATE TO THE WAITING-PLACE	127
IX.—THE GATE TO THE PHYSICIAN'S	145
X.—THE GATE TO THE CAVE	163
XI.—THE GATE TO THE SEA	181
XII.—THE GATE TO GOD'S ACRE	199
XIII.—THE GATE TO REST	215
XIV.—THE GATE TO THE HERITAGE	231
XV.—THE GATE TO THE DRILL-GROUND	247
XVI.—THE GATE TO THE HIGHLANDS	265
XVII.—THE GATE TO THE HARVEST-FIELD	283
XVIII.—THE GATE OF THE CARAVAN	299

THE ORCHARD GATE.

PSALM I.

(1) Blessed is the man who hath not walked in the counsel
   of the wicked,
   Nor stood in the way of sinners,
   Nor sat in the seat of scorners:
(2) But in the law of Jehovah is his delight,
   And in His law doth he meditate day and night.
(3) So is he like a tree planted by streams of water,
   That bringeth forth its fruit in its season,
   And whose leaf also doth not wither:
   And all that he doeth he maketh to prosper.

I.

THE ORCHARD GATE.

As one in entering a city or a public building pauses to read the inscription over the gate, so, on the threshold of this wonderful temple of song, we shall be repaid by stopping to study the first Psalm; which is a real inscription, foreshadowing what is beyond. It embodies the truth which underlies the whole Book of Psalms—that God has appointed salvation to the righteous and destruction to the wicked. Out of this theme grow the infinite modulations of aspiration, prayer, confession, personal history, denunciation, regret, praise, and admonition, which have made this book, in every age, the interpreter of the Church's deepest emotion and the favorite closet monitor of the individual saint.

The Psalm, therefore, divides itself very simply into two parts: the first treating of the character and reward of the righteous, and the second of the character and reward of the wicked.

A good man is a subject for song. He is a happy man, and happiness is contagious. He is a dispenser of strength, and comfort, and good counsel, and thus stirs up other hearts to sing. He is a struggling, but a victorious man; and victory is a theme of song the world over: and the symmetry and sweetness of the character which he develops in his struggle, are things to kindle the poet's heart, and to make men sing thanksgiving hymns for the grace which shapes a noble man in the midst of the world's pettiness and selfishness.

So it is no wonder that the Psalm breaks abruptly into our meditation with an exclamation of admiring joy:—" O, how happy is the man who shuns the path of the sinner, and delights in the law of the Lord!" It is as if the author had been long watching the panorama of human life unfolding before him in court and camp, and beholding with growing enthusiasm the course of the upright man, until, unable longer to repress his admiration, he bursts forth into words of congratulation.

The good man is first described negatively: as to what he is not; and, in this description, some have thought that a progress in evil was indicated. Thus, the good man is not one of those who begin by walking in the counsel of the ungodly; as a man who, in his walk, lounges carelessly into the company of the wicked, listening for a little while to their talk, or watching them at their pleasure. This is the "entering into temptation,"[1] against which our Lord warns us. So, consequently, the godly man avoids the second step—standing in the way of sinners; lingering in their society: and also the third, sitting in the scorner's seat—the last development of an evil career; when one has given himself wholly to the society of the wicked, has become one of them, and not only works evil, but scoffs at holiness.

There is something very suggestive in the fact that this

---

[1] Mark xiv. 38.

negative description of virtue is put first. It is true that goodness does not primarily consist in what a man is not; and the Psalm does not overlook this fact, as we shall see; but this mode of statement is based upon that assumption of the native weakness and corruption of the human heart, which underlies the whole Bible. If you are compelled to be absent from home for a day, and to leave your house in charge of a servant whom you know to be careless, and easily tempted to neglect duty—the most of your instructions are given him in this negative form. You do not so much say—" Do this, or do that," as—" Be careful that you do not forget to do this or that. Do not leave the house. Do not fail to secure the doors. Do not neglect to deliver such a message." The uppermost thought in your mind is that the servant is likely to do what he has no business to do; and against this you try to guard. The Bible assumes the same thing in the case of man. He is naturally disposed to stand in the way of sinners and to walk in the counsel of the ungodly. Of the commandments, eight begin—" Thou shalt not:" and one of the remaining two, the fourth, combines " Thou shalt" and " Thou shalt not."

But, as already observed, the Psalm does not overlook the positive side of godly character; and in presenting this, it introduces us to a charming range of thought, through a comparison with one of the most beautiful objects in nature. " He shall be like a tree planted by the rivers of water, which bringeth forth his fruit in his season. His leaf also shall not wither, and whatsoever he doeth shall prosper."

In this figure there are revealed three aspects of godly

character :—its variety, its divine culture, and its fruitfulness. Let us look at each of these in turn.

Notice the room which the figure leaves for the development of varieties of goodness. The comparison is with a fruit tree : not of any particular kind, but any one of that large class of trees ; thus giving us the whole range of the garden or the nursery from which to illustrate the infinite diversity with which moral beauty and fruitfulness reveal themselves. True godliness does not reduce men to a dead level. The variety which God stamps upon nature, He means to have reproduced in character. It is often supposed that, by becoming a servant of God, a man loses all his distinctiveness, sacrifices many of his peculiar modes of power, and shuts himself up to a comparatively narrow range of activity : whereas the truth is that no man ever finds out the variety of uses to which human talent and power can be put, until he begins to work under God's direction. Neither the variety nor the measure of power are fully developed until then. The power and the opportunity are never in contact until then. There is no grade of talent, no acquirement, no odd individuality, no natural gift, no trained faculty, for which the kingdom of grace has not fifty places and modes of exercise where the kingdom of nature has one : and one reason why the human race presents so many of what we call oddities of character, is because these are out of the place which God made for them. When a thing is in its place, it ceases to be odd. A man who had never seen a gun, might take up the various parts of it as they lay on the workman's bench, and declare that he could not conceive why such things should ever have been made ; that curiously shaped piece of wood; that clicking lock, working back and forth so oddly; that long iron tube—what are they all for? He finds out when the gunsmith puts lock, stock, and barrel together, and the sportsman charges the piece and brings down with it the bounding deer. Hundreds of men and women are in contact with society like tenons which have no socket. They are protuberances which press against society, and irritate it, and make, by dint of much rubbing, a kind of ill-fitting place for themselves. Let God once put such people in *His* places, and all the tenons find their sockets.

A man once called upon me who had been rescued from the depths of ruffianism, and who was carrying on a mission among the outcasts in the lower wards of the city. He was telling of the prayer-meetings they held there; and how they were not unfrequently disturbed by drunken rioters, who broke into the room and had to be put out by force. Said he: "When anything of that kind happens, they just strike up a hymn, and I go as quietly as I can and get them out of the room. Sometimes they are very ugly and strike at me. But you know I was a fighting man myself once, and pretty well used to taking care of myself with my hands; *and its astonishing how handy it comes now.*" The illustration is all the better, because it comes from so low down. God had a place for the mere brute power and training which had made a ruffian a pest of society, and could turn it to use, on occasion, for the protection of His own house and worship.

The comparison farther illustrates the divine culture of godly character. The godly man is not like a tree which grows wild. He is like a tree planted, and that in a place which will best promote its growth. Godly character is developed under God's special supervision, and with God's own appliances. We cannot but notice here how our Savior's words are anticipated: " Ye have not chosen me, but I have chosen you, and *planted* you,[1] that ye should bring forth fruit and that your fruit should remain." And it is no small thing, in a world where so many are out of their place, or without any place at all, to be assured that any man who chooses may do his work and develop his character in a place of God's choosing. We think perhaps it would be a great thing for us to have our place pointed out as clearly as Moses' or Paul's. Well, why not ? Was it only for a dozen men that the promise was made, that any man who lacks wisdom can have it by asking of God in faith ? Has God no other means of revealing His will, but through a burning bush or a stunning shock ? On the contrary, His modes of revelation are as many as the characters and circumstances of men, and as varied; and He does not mean that His lowliest servant shall work under the shadow of a doubt whether he is in his place or not. He may make circumstances, or conscientious judgment, or special dispensations His messengers, but whatever be the messenger, the message shall be clear to the open eye and the obedient spirit—" I have planted you."

And if a man is working and growing where God sets him, he is always within reach of the means necessary for his growth and fruitfulness. He is always planted by rivers of water. Men find these channels in the most un-

---

[1] Such is the true rendering of "*ordained,*" John xv. 16.

likely places; in the most unpromising parts of God's garden. In their very work they find something to engage their energy, quicken their enthusiasm, and develop their power. It is wonderful what grand trees will often grow up among rocks;[1] and what majesty of character and variety and reach of power will often be nourished by hardship. One would naturally have supposed that Paul's imprisonment was the end of his missionary career; yet it was one of the most fruitful periods of his life to the Christian Church of all time. Not to speak of his work in the imperial household, the fruit of his being planted in that seemingly barren spot, drops rich and ripe into the Church's hand to-day from the Philippian, Colossian, and Ephesian epistles, and from the little letter to Philemon.

And this is a mystery to men of the world. They look

---

[1] "The resources of trees," says Ruskin, "are not developed until they have difficulty to contend with; neither their tenderness of brotherly love and harmony, till they are forced to choose their ways of various life where there is contracted room for them, talking to each other with their restrained branches. The various action of trees rooting themselves in inhospitable rocks, stooping to look into ravines, hiding from the search of glacier winds, reaching forth to the rays of rare sunshine, crowding down together to drink at sweetest streams, climbing hand in hand among the difficult slopes, opening in sudden dances round the mossy knolls, gathering into companies at rest among the fragrant fields, gliding in grave procession over the homeward ridges—nothing of this can be conceived among the unvexed and unvaried felicities of the lowland forest."

And Heinrich Heine, in his "Harzreise," has a similar thought. "They" (the mountain trees) "stand firmer than their comfortable colleagues in the cultivated forest ground of the lowland. Thus in life stand those great men who, through victory over earlier hindrances and obstacles, have won strength and steadfastness."

at the places in which some of God's servants are planted, and say it is impossible they should bear fruit there. Circumstances are all against them. There are no capabilities in the place. They must go away, or they will starve, mentally and spiritually, aye, and bodily too; and yet they do not starve, and they are not crushed. Amid sickness, bereavement, scant opportunities, hatred, scorn, they not only live, but grow, and have something to spare for other lives,—yea, minister to them most richly and effectively. What is more, they themselves are cheerful and strong, and grow in sweetness no less than in power. It is a mystery to the world, I say, but no mystery to him who knows this Psalm by heart. "The secret of the Lord is with them that fear Him."[1] Even so have I seen a tree standing out in a dreary, stony plain, under the blazing sun, yet fresh and green, and with the stir of life in its leaves and branches; and that though I could see no gleam of water, and hear the gurgle of no stream through the stillness of the shimmering noon. Yet none the less was it planted by the waters. Down deep under the soil flowed the rills which bathed its roots and nourished its life. And the waters by which God feeds these planted lives of His in dry places are seldom seen. They flow in deep channels of God's digging, where the eye of man cannot track them, but where they run, charged with strength and gladness, to the souls which are weary and heavy laden. Do you know where this truth finds its highest illustration? Did you ever ponder that wonderful text in the Epistle to the Hebrews? "It became Him for whom are all things,

---

[1] Ps. xxv. 14.

and by whom are all things, in bringing many sons into glory, to make the Captain of their salvation perfect through suffering."[1] What do those words mean, but that suffering is God's mightiest instrument of perfection? What is the meaning of the life and agony and death of the Man of sorrows, but to show to an incredulous world—a world which believes that suffering can only blight, that the rarest, grandest humanity the world has ever seen or ever will see, could grow up in the hardest and most barren soil in which humanity ever struggled for life?

And Christian men, yet of little faith, not unfrequently find this a mystery too. You find one here and there who doubts whether God planted him because he cannot see the rivers of water. He says—" I should be more fruitful if I were planted somewhere else; if I were not confined to this sick-bed; if I could go to church or to prayer-meeting oftener; if I were in a less worldly atmosphere."

It is very, very doubtful. If God has planted you, there is a river of water somewhere near you; and you can do no better thing, nothing half so good as to find the river on your ground. That is the stream adapted to strengthen your peculiar weakness, and to nourish your peculiar form of power. You are much on a sick-bed. You wish you might be planted on some healthful height in God's garden. But God has set you among the chill damps, and the fever heats, and in the languid air which swoons with lassitude; but there is a stream called Patience flowing close by that sick-bed, and it may be that God put you there for nothing else but to find it. You

---

[1] Heb. ii. 10.

miss the stimulus and the inspiration of social worship; it may have been, in olden days, when you were in the whirl of society, something kept you at home for awhile; and you learned in that interval to know a true friend whose worth you never knew before; and so it may be that Christ wanted to show you how much He could be to you; and He drew you aside all to Himself, planted you where He alone could tend you, and if you have found your river, you know now, as you never knew before, the meaning of those words—"He that drinketh of the water that I shall give him shall never thirst; but the water that I shall give him shall be in him, a well of water, springing up into everlasting life." [1] And thus it is with all the bare spots where God plants you. If *He* plants you, it is always by rivers of water. See that you find your river in your place. Though you miss the sweet companionship which has lightened your years of toil, though the sun of sorrow seem to dry up every drop of refreshing, though your iron ring hard against the cruel rock, yet search, for you shall find living water by and by. Not very long ago I received a letter from a friend who had been passing through eight long months of weary watching and anxious dread, and toil, robbed of all heart by the lowering shadow of possible bereavement. He said—"I believe more than ever in prayer in the closet." Those eight months wrote their mark upon him, but he found his river; and when a man strikes that water—prayer, he goes down to an artesian well, deep as the being of God, and exhaustless as eternity.

---

[1] John iv. 14.

Fruitfulness is the natural result of all this. God's tree by God's river must be a fruitful tree. "He that abideth in Me, and I in him, the same bringeth forth much fruit."[1] "Those that be planted in the courts of the Lord, shall flourish in the courts of our God."[2] Only we must note two little hints in this verse, either of which might easily be expanded into a sermon. The first is—"*his* fruit;" not any other tree's fruit. God gives the tree its nature, and plants it where it can best develop its nature, and looks for fruit according to its nature and place. So, after you have done your best work in the place where God has set you, do not be disturbed and irritated because it is not the rarer, more beautiful work of some other man. No man's vanity ought to be kindled by his work; but he who casts contempt on his own honest work, when he has done his best as unto God, insults God, no matter if his work be inferior to that of ten thousand other men. You are not to waste time in admiring or envying other men's modes of power, but to give your whole energy to the development of your own mode of power. And if your best is only a single fruit—why, many a time I have seen a gardener point with special pride and pleasure to a dwarf pear-tree which had gathered up its whole little life into one single pear; and if your life's best labor brings to pass but a single result, go back to the thought —God planted me — and be well content, as you will have a right to be, with the inference from that; He planted me that I might do that one thing. The whole Christian Church to-day is suffering because of the multi-

---

[1] John xv. 5.   [2] Ps. xcii. 13.

tude of its members who are doing nothing because they cannot do what somebody else does.

And the other hint is in the words—"In his season." The seasons are different for different fruits. Some are early, some are late. And likewise moral growths do not all fructify at the same time or rate. No workman of God need be disheartened because his fruit season comes late, any more than the luscious pear of the late Autumn need fold up its leaves and die, because its fruit was hard and green in the earlier weeks, when the harvest-apples hung ripe and juicy from their boughs. The latest fruit is usually the best. But, early or late, the fruit of godly character is seasonable. It will be found that God nourishes His men as He does the fruits of the earth, to meet the demands of special seasons; and that in each individual character divine graces fructify as the occasion demands;—courage for seasons of danger, patience for seasons of suffering, strength for seasons of trial, wisdom for seasons of difficulty, words spoken in season—in short, the beautiful fitness of godliness is no less remarkable than its fruitfulness.

"And whatsoever he doeth shall prosper." This is a kind of general summary of the condition which, thus far, has been treated in detail. It is a most astonishing promise to give to men; yet here, as all through this Psalm, the correspondence with the broader thought of the New Testament is marked. "All things are yours"[1] because you are God's. Whatsoever he doeth shall prosper, because he is planted in God's garden, by God's rivers.

---

[1] 1 Cor. iii. 21.

Only, this suggests a very important thought as to the standard of prosperity. If it is prosperity which comes from God, it must be measured by God's rule—and I need not say that that is quite another rule from men's— so that, with reference to a large number of godly men, the world is disposed to deny this statement and to say it is rather the other way : whatsoever he doeth does *not* prosper. He has sickness and financial disaster; his plans miscarry; he has tribulation, distress, nakedness and peril. Yet it by no means follows that he does not prosper according to a different and a higher standard.

I stood last summer in a magnificent hothouse, where the luscious clusters of grapes were all around and above ; and the owner said, " When my new gardener came, he said he would have nothing to do with these vines unless he could cut them clear down to the stock ; and he did, and we had no grapes for two years ; but this is the result." It did not look much like fruit when the stocks stood bare and the floor was heaped with cuttings ; but the gardener looked over the two years, and saw what we were seeing and tasting. And thus we naturally turn to our Savior's words—" Every branch in Me which beareth fruit, He purgeth it that it may bring forth more fruit."[1] God prunes the trees in His own garden, and Faith looks away from the stock which seems so cruelly cut down, and sees the riches of coming years. Any one can see, at a glance, how Paul has learned this lesson, when he says of tribulation, and distress, and peril—" Nay, *in* all

---

[1] John xv. 2.

these things we are abundantly the conquerors through Him that loved us." [1]

And now let us look for a moment at the great supply which nourishes these trees of God and these fruits of holiness. Why is the godly life at once so fruitful and so delightsome? "His delight is in the law of the Lord; and in His law doth he meditate day and night." This is the stream from which all the minor streams flow: that which gives character to all the juices which promote the growth of godliness. From the law of God all the comforts and incentives, all the warnings and injunctions which go to make man better and more efficient, take their rise and acquire their flavor. He delights in it because he loves its Author. Men do not naturally love law They rebel at restraint, and court what they call freedom; and no man can ever love law in itself. A code has no power to inspire love. He will love the law only through the lawgiver. He will delight in a law which restrains and prunes him, only as he takes supreme delight in the Author of the law. He will meditate on it because he delights in it, as we always think on that which we love; and only through meditating on it will he grow and be fruitful. Meditation is to religious growth, what the drawing up of the juices into the fibres is to the growth of the tree. We make a great mistake if we carry the law into our seasons of activity only. We do indeed learn much of its practical power and value in that way, but a large share of its beauty and richness unfolds only in our hours of retirement, when we

---

[1] Rom. viii. 37.

commune with our hearts upon our beds and are still. You have been in a greenhouse, and have seen the large petals of the night-blooming cereus closely folded together, as if shrinking from the stir and bustle of the day; but as the hours of the night passed away, little by little they fell apart, and the great blossom spread out its creamy leaves to the breath of the night, and made the air heavy with its fragrance. And so it is with the law of God. It may be in a man's heart, yet the crowd of the day's duties and cares may press round it so as to hide its beauty and partially to stifle its fragrance; but in the hours when thought is free to dwell upon its cherished themes, under the power of midnight meditation it expands and discloses new beauties and sweeter perfume, until the delighted servant of God cries—" O how love I thy law!" [1]

The great lesson, then, of this first part of the Psalm is, —Holiness is happiness, security, stability, fruitfulness: and holiness is based solely upon the law of God. Within the sphere of that law, as in a sheltered and well-watered garden, are all the fountains which minister to perfect blessedness and to permanent efficiency. Prosperity! That is what we all are seeking. Are we sure that we know what true prosperity is? We need be in no doubt if we but get by heart the lesson of this Psalm. It is being in God's ground, placed by God's hand, fed by God's supplies. Stability! Something fixed and settled! It has been the craving of the world in all ages; its cry through all its restlessness and shifting. Its cry is heard

---

[1] Ps. cxix. 97.

and answered here. He is fixed indeed whom God plants in His own ground, and makes steadfast and immovable. Security! How much fear and quaking are there in human hearts. What a yearning for some safe place of rest. Let the Psalmist lead you to the safest of all places—the garden of God, beside the rivers of His peace. What poisonous breath shall infect that tree? What blast overthrow it? What hand wound it, while it grows within God's enclosure? "He that dwelleth in the secret place of the Most High, shall abide under the shadow of the Almighty."[1] Fruitfulness! We are ambitious, full of the spirit of active work. God takes us into His garden to use and to develop our enthusiasm, yet also to tone down our ambition, and to teach us the nature of true success. If He teach us to work, we shall be workmen that need not to be ashamed. If He give us success, our success will stand the fiery trial of His judgment seat, and will "be found unto praise and honor and glory at the appearing of Jesus Christ."[2] Let us follow the Psalmist gladly into the garden of God's law; and as we revel in its beauty and refreshment, may we be prompted to say, "This is my rest forever. Here will I dwell, for I have desired it."[3]

---

[1] Ps. xci. 1.   [2] 1 Pet. i. 7.   [3] Ps. cxxxii. 14.

THE GATE TO THE THRESH-
ING-FLOOR.

PSALM I.—(*Continued*.)

(4) Not so are the wicked;
 But they are like the chaff which the wind driveth away.

(5) Therefore the wicked shall not stand in the judgment;
 Nor sinners in the congregation of the righteous.

(6) For Jehovah knoweth the way of the righteous,
 And the way of the wicked shall perish.

II.

THE GATE TO THE THRESHING-FLOOR.

THIS is not as pleasant a theme as the last. Yet if we would see the word of God in its unity, we must face the shadows as well as the lights. And as, in nature, you have observed that nothing is more sharply defined than the edge of a shadow, so here, there is no gradual merging of one class of characters into another. There is no intimation here of any middle ground between godliness and ungodliness. Here and elsewhere, the Bible ranges men on either side of a strongly marked line. Either they are planted by God's hand in God's garden, beside God's streams, or they are outside the enclosure. Christ deals with this matter in the same way. He throws men into two categories: those who are with Him and those who are against Him; "and he that is not with Him is against Him; and he that gathereth not with Him scattereth abroad."[1] Paul, too, when he speaks of the masters to which man may yield himself, recognizes only two. "To whom ye yield yourselves servants to obey, his servants ye are to whom ye obey, whether of sin unto death, or of obedience unto righteousness."[2] And since this truth underlies the entire Psalm, and the entire Bible for that

---

[1] Matt. xii. 30. [2] Rom. vi. 16.

matter, it ought to be clearly understood. No one pretends that every man who is not an avowed servant of God is a defier of all moral obligation. No one denies that such often exhibit the loveliest moral traits; but the question is broader than this, and concerns the moral administration under which each man lives. An American citizen may go and live for years in Paris. He may speak the French language well, dress like those around him, and be, in no outward respect, distinguishable from a native Parisian; and yet he may acknowledge no allegiance to the French Government. When a decisive issue arises which compels him to declare himself, you find him at the American minister's, under the protection of his own flag.

And God's tests, in like manner, go straight through these superficial developments of character, down to the roots of character. Where is it planted? Whence does it get its impulse? What gives it its ultimate law? Under what administration is it? Where are you a citizen? The Bible will not stop to discuss with you the advantages of a foreign administration, nor its points of resemblance to God's administration, nor the eligibleness or respectability of your position elsewhere. The Bible is on God's side, and is concerned only with the question of allegiance to God. It puts us to this simple test—citizen or foreigner? God's servant or not? That NOT contains the germs of all moral disaster.

Thus we are prepared for the sharp contrast with which this lesson is introduced: "The ungodly are NOT SO." The Psalmist does not dwell upon the details of their ungodliness. As in the case of the righteous, he confines himself to indicating the sources of their life, and passes over all that intervenes, until the judgment. The great object of this introductory Psalm is to show us *the fountain heads* of moral character. Its developments of both kinds we find in abundance throughout the Book of Psalms; but in this the proper truth to be set forth, is the fundamental one, that all true fruitfulness of character is found in God's garden only; in being planted by God's hand and by God's rivers, and that all barrenness and uselessness result from being NOT SO.

Let us then look at some of the aspects of the character which is not so. This too is set forth by a figure. We have seen the flourishing tree. The garden enclosure shuts it in; the watercourses bathe its roots; the leaf is green, and the fruit hangs thick and tempting. We leave now the garden gate, and not far off behold a raised platform of earth beaten hard. It is the threshing floor. Here stand the workmen with their earthen vessels, and scooping up the threshed grain mingled with chaff, throw it up into the air, or let it fall in a stream from the uplifted jar; and the wind, with its whirling gusts which arise so suddenly on the plains, catches the chaff and drives it away before it. "The ungodly are like the chaff which the wind driveth away;"—light, shifting, worthless.

We have then set forth under this figure three aspects of the ungodly character;—its instability, its worthlessness, its insecurity.

One of the happiest phases of goodness is its fixedness. Not that stubborn obstinacy which certain really upright men seem to feel it their duty to cultivate, but a stability which consists with a good degree of flexibility, and with the very largest fruitfulness : such a steadfastness and immovableness as always abounds in the work of the Lord, and which is therefore well represented by a tree, firmly rooted, moving with the breath of the wind, and shaking down fruit as it moves. A life rooted thus in God, is based on settled conviction, has a single aim, a uniform tendency, and a permanent result. In these particulars the opposite character fails. As to rational conviction, when a man ceases to believe in God and in God's law, what is he not likely to believe ? Theory after theory comes rolling in from the great deep of speculation, and he is borne now upon one billow, now upon another, and again is out of sight in the trough of the sea. Take a life away from God, and you take from it unity of impulse. Passion, pride, selfishness, drive it hither and thither as the winds drive the dismantled ship. Nowhere but in God does man find a consistent law. The laws which he makes for himself have all sorts of accommodating curves round his pet desires. They are cushioned and padded where they bear upon his favorite indulgences. It is only the statutes of the Lord which are right— *straight*, rejoicing the heart. Consequently, such a life has no singleness of aim. Its aims are as varied as its impulses. It moves toward as many points as the driven chaff ; now toward sensual, now toward intellectual gratification ; now toward fame, now toward wealth. It is an uneasy life, vague alike in its desires and in its hopes, with no well-defined point of rest in view. And O, that men would learn the lesson of this uneasiness ; for it has a lesson for them. Even as the flying chaff, whirled on before the rapid wind, tells that somewhere there is ripe grain, and harvest to be garnered, so this unrest, this ever-recurring thirst of the soul, is a reminder of its home in God. In the beautiful words of Augustine, "Thou madest us for Thyself, and our heart is restless until it repose in Thee."

The second phase of this character is its worthlessness. Chaff! The wind drives it away and the husbandman is glad to have it driven away. Here again we find ourselves in the track of Gospel thought. "Every tree which bringeth not forth good fruit, is hewn down and cast into the fire."[1] "Every plant which my Heavenly Father hath not planted, shall be rooted up:"[2] rooted up for no other reason than that He hath not planted it; and that though it be green and apparently fruitful. So that we cannot evade the plain proposition—An ungodly life is a worthless life because, whatever it may be, however bustling and busy, it is NOT SO. It is not used under God's direction and for God's uses. Even in worldly matters, men are often deceived by a busy life. They see a man who is always active, who talks a great deal about how much he has to do, who does everything with much bustle and stir, and they insensibly come to regard him as a most important and useful man, when in fact he may be neither.

The present age is very susceptible to this fallacy—the identification of activity with usefulness. It is counted high praise to say of one — "He is industrious; he is never idle; therefore he is a good member of society." And the Bible outdoes the world in its praises of faithful

---

[1] Matthew iii. 10. [2] Matthew xv. 13.

labor, and in its stinging words for the drone; but it has no praise for work in itself considered. It goes below the work and asks—"Under whose direction? For what? For whom?" And it calls that man useful who works on God's lines and in God's way, for God's ends; and it gathers into one category as useless all who are NOT SO. Is that unreasonable? A general pitches his tent near a green meadow, and sends out a sergeant for recruits. Day after day the officer comes in with new volunteers, and they are ordered into line and put under training. But pretty soon comes along a party of men with scythes on their shoulders. "Come! Don't you want to enlist? There is special and honorable service before us, and the state wants its ranks filled quickly." "Well, General," replies one, "you may consider us enlisted, if you like. We are willing to serve the state; and so we have come to mow this meadow." "But I don't care whether the meadow is mowed or not. I want men to handle muskets, not scythes." "No, we prefer to mow; You shall see how active we will be; how the long swaths will go down before us." Will any one blame the General because he says of those fine stalwart fellows, so eager to work, so active—"They are useless?" What else can he say? He wants men for *war;* ready and able to fight, and whatever they may be, they are useless if they are NOT SO. It is not enough that you are what society calls useful, what your family calls useful, what even the Church calls useful. The main, the only test of your usefulness applies to its moral relations. If you are not working under God's orders, your greatest apparent usefulness may be a power for evil. A great deal of what passes here for honest work, aye, for Christian work, will be summarily thrown out at the day of judgment, leaving the man who has been so busy, with his work for his pains.

Useless! Nay, there is a sense in which such a man is useful. God makes use of him, against his will, to serve His own divine purpose.

"Blindly the wicked work the righteous will of heaven."

But what a lot for an immortal soul, for a divinely created will :—to be used because it cannot help it. To become useful through its destruction, like the ashes of the fruitless vines, which enrich the soil and make other vines heavy with the fruit which they refuse to bear. O, for a soul to have been useless in the thick crowd of such noble uses : useless, in the face of work which might have enlisted the enthusiasm of angels : useless, when there were so many calls for its power : useless, when Heaven was ready to charge it with its own energy, and to set it moving on a track of conquest. To have God look down with contempt on the bustling activity on which it was wont to pride itself, and upon the objects on which it expended its strength, and say, "To what purpose is this waste?" and to drive the soul which thought itself so important and so useful, like useless chaff before the breath of His indignation.

There will come a time when those who have lived for self and have looked upon life only as a means of ministering to their pride, and ease, and pleasure, will get a new and startling view of the dignity of ministry, of the surpassing blessedness of a life ministering in Christ's name, and therewith a painful sense of the utter uselessness of the life which comes to be ministered unto; which receives all, and gives nothing. It is only the grain, which gives itself to be broken and kneaded, the grain, which falls into the ground and dies to multiply itself and to feed the famishing—only the *grain* which is hoarded. The chaff, which only lives by the grain, which feeds no one, which has no power of reproduction, is driven away. So it is the law, the unchanging law of God, that the life which gives nothing has no place in His divine order; that the life which is bound to no other life by God's laws of love and of ministry, but is self-centred, is a light, useless life, to be shaken to the four winds when God shall shake heaven and earth. I know not but this picture gave direction to the lurid imagination of the great Italian poet, when he painted the eternal doom of those who subjugate reason to appetite, in that place

"Mute of all light,
Which bellows as the sea does in a tempest,"

and where

" The infernal hurricane that never rests
Hurtles the spirits onward in its rapine :
Whirling them round and smiting, it molests them :

And as the wings of starlings bear them on
In the cold season, in large band and full,
So doth that blast the spirits maledict :
It hither, thither, downward, upward, drives them :
No hope doth comfort them for evermore,
Not of repose but even of lesser pain." [1]

---

[1] Dante, "Inferno," Canto V., Longfellow's Trans.

And with such a picture before us, I need not dwell upon the insecurity of the ungodly. The contrast is obvious between the tree, safe in its enclosure by the watercourses, watched and tended by the gardener, its fruits safe from the plunderer—and the chaff, loosely lying on the exposed threshing floor, where the first blast can drive it, no one cares whither. How safe is the man who abides in God; while he who puts himself outside of the restraints of divine law, forfeits likewise its protection.

And this thought of the insecurity of the ungodly furnishes a transition point to the next section of the Psalm, which turns on the truth that the real weakness and instability of the character which is not founded in God's law shall finally be made manifest. The whole current of the Psalm moves in the direction of a day of final tests which shall lay bare the foundations of character. All the obscurity which now beclouds the conditions and mutual relations of the righteous and of the wicked, shall be done away. As things now are, this obscurity is very oppressive. The ungodly man often appears the more prosperous and the safer man of the two. He is compassed about with friends, secure in popularity, well furnished with wealth. He seems to be well grounded. The "green bay tree" lifts up its head outside the garden enclosure, and towers higher than the fruit-tree within, and spreads its branches in great power. Again we find ourselves in the track of our Saviour's thought; and, singularly enough, under the same figure. This part of the Psalm is an almost literal anticipation of the parable of the tares.[1] Tares and wheat are in the same field, as

---

[1] Matthew xii. 24, 30.

wheat and chaff are on the same threshing-floor. The tares, for the time, enjoy immunity for the wheat's sake: are not summarily rooted up lest the wheat be rooted up with them. So the chaff, while it keeps close to the wheat, enjoys some privileges for the wheat's sake. In the world, good and evil grow together. They often look so much alike that no human eye can distinguish them. Evil takes advantage of good for its own ends. Scores of the immunities and privileges enjoyed by evil men, which make them tolerable and respectable, and even influential in the society in which they move, yea, which enable them to concoct their schemes, and to practice their hypocrisies, and to deceive the world with their superficial morality, are the outgrowths of the very good at which they mock, and of the very principles which they defy. Meanwhile both grow together. The blunder of the world which mistakes wheat for tares and tares for wheat is permitted, for God's reasons, to perpetuate itself for the time. The wicked "stands in the congregation of the righteous." The wolf walks undetected in sheep's clothing. The malicious persecutor triumphs. The godly man is slandered, and his name blackened, and his power lamed. Worldly prosperity is not apportioned according to desert. "Is it always," as one happily puts it, "the swift who win the race, and the strong who carry off the honors of the battle? Do none of our intelligent lack bread, nor any of the learned favor? Are there no fools lifted to high places, to show with how little wisdom the world is governed, and no noble, heroic breasts dinted by the blows of hostile circumstance, or wounded by 'the slings and arrows of outrageous fortune?' Are there none in our midst who have to bear

> 'The whips and scorns of time,
> The oppressor's wrong, the proud man's contumely,
> The pangs of despised love, the law's delay,
> The insolence of office, and the spurns
> That patient merit of the unworthy takes'?"[1]

Alas, it is only in romances that virtue always triumphs, and vice always goes under. In short, it is the old problem which has tasked the minds of sober thinkers from the beginning of time, and has driven some of them well-nigh to despair—the problem stated by Job: "Wherefore do the wicked live, become old, yea, are mighty in power? Their seed is established in their sight with them, and their offspring before their eyes. Their houses are safe from fear, neither is the rod of God upon them."[2] Similarly, the old Preacher breathes the note of despair as he looks. "So I returned and considered all the oppressions that are done under the sun, and behold, the tears of such as were oppressed, and they had no comforter: and on the side of their oppressors there was power; but they had no comforter. Wherefore I praised the dead which are already dead more than the living which are yet alive."[3]

---

[1] Samuel Cox, "The Quest of the Chief Good."
[2] Job xxi. 7–9.
[3] Eccles. iv. 1–2. Compare Sophocles, Œdipus at Colonos, 1226.
> "Happiest beyond compare
> Never to taste of life;
> Happiest in order next,
> Being born, with quickest speed
> Thither again to turn

But our Psalm does not leave us here. It carries us over this time of the growing together of wheat and tares, to the time of separation. It leads our eye through all the confusion and contradiction, to a settled point of rest. There is coming a day of judgment whose searching tests shall resolve the confusion, and make clearly manifest to the world what is weak and what is strong; what is solid and what is superficial; what is wheat and what is chaff. The preacher who sounds that despairing note that death is better than life with this problem unsolved, fights his way through the billows and reaches land at last, and leaves us with the words—" God shall bring every work into judgment with every secret thing, whether it be good or whether it be evil."[1] And Job does not go on long in the strain of one hopelessly baffled by the spectacle of the wicked man's prosperity. A few verses more and the note changes. " How oft is the candle of the wicked put out, and how oft cometh their destruction upon them. God distributeth sorrows in His anger. They are as stubble before the wind, and as chaff that the storm carrieth away."[2]

And here we find ourselves viewing the judgment in a mood which, I suspect, is not habitual with us. In our ordinary thoughts on the judgment we are chiefly occupied with its terrors. We shrink from its fiery trial. Fear of

---

      From whence we came.
      When youth hath passed away,
      With all its follies light,
      What sorrow is not there ? "
              —PLUMPTRE'S TRANS.

[1] Eccles. xii. 14.   [2] Job xxi. 17, 18.

its searching tests is our uppermost feeling; and we sing

"That Day of wrath, that dreadful Day!"

and

"That awful Day will surely come."

I do not dispute the propriety of these expressions; but with all its terror, it has another side. "There was a time in the first flush of Christian faith, when the second coming was daily, hourly expected: when the believers looked little to the future, and fancied that the ministry of Jesus Christ had been but the beginning of the end;" and, if I do not misinterpret the sentiment of those early apostolic times concerning the judgment, it was a joyful, hopeful sentiment rather than one of terror. It was the coming of the Lord to redeem and glorify His people, and to vindicate His struggling church; and we get into much the same mood through the study of the awful problem on which we have touched. That is the dominant feeling of the book of Ecclesiastes, which deals with this problem of human life. If it be true that this book was composed during the later captivity, under the Persian administration, it is easy to imagine how a Hebrew exile would look forward to a day of judgment. The slave of a luxurious despot's whims, afraid to accumulate property lest it should tempt the rapacity of some powerful courtier, liable to be put to death at any moment to gratify the passing fancy of the monarch, or to have the whole circle of his kindred cut off at the breath of a malicious slander,[1] in daily contact with the arbitrary system or absence of system which rewarded incompe-

---

[1] As in the case of Mordecai.

tency, raised worthlessness, and degraded merit—we can imagine, I say, how the thought of a judgment would be to such a man the most welcome of all thoughts; and can appreciate thus the undertone of triumph in the concluding words of the book,—" God shall bring every work into judgment with every secret thing." And this feeling creeps into our Psalm; intimated rather than pronounced in the words, "the Lord knoweth the way of the righteous." A dark way it has been sometimes. A way which has made men question the profitableness of godliness. A way under the shadow of a cross, and compassed about by the phantoms of the pit; yet God has known all its windings, and has known that through darkness it led up to Him, just as He has known that other way which lay so high, and broad, and smooth under the full blaze of prosperity's sun, and has seen its end in a precipice, over which the prosperous sinner shall be swept like chaff. Therefore, I repeat, we have a right to draw consolation no less than caution and godly fear from the judgment. It will be a comfort to have this fearful problem of the long tolerated commingling of tares and wheat decisively solved; and that in a way which shall vindicate the wisdom and the justice of a God to whom His people cling, though He hide Himself in clouds: which shall prove the eternal solidity of those principles of action to which they hold against all dictates of worldly policy: which shall right all wrongs and riddle all shams, and bring to naught all vain boasting, and set each man in his true place as related to God. A comfort this to God's servants, but no less a terror to the wicked. O, what a fearful winnowing shall swell the chaff heaps in that day. What hypocrisies shall be disengaged from their goodly wrappings: what self-deceptions blown naked from their shelter into the remorseless light: what imposing phantoms of greatness and usefulness and goodness driven away like morning mist. "The ungodly shall not stand in the judgment."

Here then is the contrast between the two portions of this Psalm. Here is the fruitful, cherished tree, and here the driving chaff. On the one side, stability, divine culture, fruitfulness; on the other, instability, uselessness, ruin. On the one side, a law which nourishes every form of goodly power, and provides every variety of instruction and of comfort; on the other, license which dissipates power, begets restlessness, and ends in worthlessness. On the one side, a divine vindication, on the other a divine exposure. Which shall be our portion? Where our place? In the garden beside the river of God, or on the threshing floor at the mercy of the wind?

THE ORATORY GATE.

PSALM V.

(1) Give ear to my words, O Jehovah,
 Consider my meditation.
(2) Hearken unto the voice of my cry, my King and my God,
 For unto Thee do I pray.
(3) Jehovah, in the morning shalt Thou hear my voice,
 In the morning will I set in order for Thee (my prayer) and watch.
(4) For Thou art not a God that hath pleasure in wickedness,
 Evil cannot sojourn with Thee.
(5) Fools cannot stand in Thy sight;
 Thou hatest all workers of iniquity.
(6) Thou destroyest them that speak lies;
 The bloodthirsty and deceitful man doth Jehovah abhor.
(7) But as for me—in the multitude of Thy loving kindness will I enter Thy house;
 I will bow myself towards Thy holy temple in Thy fear.
(8) O Jehovah, lead me in Thy righteousness, because of them that lie in wait for me,
 Make Thy way plain before my face;
(9) For there is no faithfulness in their mouth;
 Their inward part is a yawning gulf;
 Their throat is an open sepulchre,
 (While) they make smooth their tongue.
(10) Punish Thou them, O God :—
 Let them fall through their own counsels :
 In the multitude of their transgressions thrust them away;
 For they have rebelled against Thee.
(11) And all who find refuge in Thee shall rejoice;
 Forever shall they shout for joy;
 And Thou wilt defend them;
 And they who love Thy name shall exult in Thee.
(12) For Thou, O Jehovah, dost bless the righteous,
 With favor dost Thou compass him as with a shield.

III.

THE ORATORY GATE.

"It is certain," says Robert Leighton, "that the greater part of men, as they babble out vain, languid, and inefficacious prayers, most unworthy of the ear of the blessed God, so they seem, in some degree, to set a just estimate upon them, neither hoping for any success from them, nor indeed seeming to be at all solicitous about it, but committing them to the wind as vain words, which in truth they are."

It is indeed a serious thing when prayer is thus abused; but the abuse is committed in the face of very plain lessons in the word of God. No reader of that word need ignorantly degrade this most solemn and sublime act of a human soul.

Such a lesson is this Psalm. It is a prayer itself; and while the subject-matter of the prayer is of great interest, the Psalm is peculiar in setting forth the characteristics of prayer in general. In this aspect let us study it.

We have, in the first place, in the first and second verses, a suggestion of the *variety* of prayer—" Give ear to my *words :*" *formal* prayer. " Consider my *meditation :*" *unexpressed* prayer. " Hearken unto my *cry :* " *ejaculatory* prayer. Prayer is a provision for a universal need, and must therefore be capable of a large variety of adaptations.

It is for the dumb no less than for him who speaks; for sudden emergencies no less than for stated occasions; for the closet, but also for the crowd. If a man is to pray without ceasing, he must pray under an endless variety of circumstances. Thus we have here suggested a season when prayer can be deliberately uttered. When one's desires can frame themselves into words; when he can follow the periods of carefully worded liturgies, or pour out a free heart in spontaneous speech. Then we have that which is equally prayer, denoted by the word meditation; that which lies in the heart as unexpressed desire or aspiration; which indicates a state or habit of mind quite as much as an act.

"Meditation," says Gurnall, "is prayer in bullion: prayer in the ore—soon melted and run into holy desires." The value of prayer does not lie in its demonstrativeness. On the contrary, the soul's unexpressed aspiration is often more truly prayer than the well-rounded formula. We should be especially careful to distinguish between the *spirit* and the *habit* of prayer. The habit may exist without the spirit; but the spirit will always beget the habit. The spirit can be the result only of the life of God in the soul; the habit of prayer may be the result of education merely.

Then we have a third of the many varieties of prayer suggested by the word "*cry:*"—the passionate outburst of a soul in distress, or dejection, or danger; throwing out a prayer like a strongly shot dart,[1] which gives to such prayer the name of *ejaculatory*. "These darts may

---

[1] Jaculum.

be shot to heaven without using the tongue's bow. Such a kind of prayer that of Moses was, which rang so loud in God's ear that He asked him—'Wherefore criest thou unto Me?' Whereas we do not read of a word that he spake."[1] Or such may be the mere inarticulate cry of a soul which knows not what it should pray for as it ought:

> "So runs my dream, but what am I?
> An infant crying in the night:
> An infant crying for the light,
> And with no language but a cry."

And it is worth noting that such a prayer as this links itself closely with meditation. It can proceed only from a true spirit of prayer so far as that is indicated by a genuine sense of need. Such prayer is always genuine. It is wrung from men in times when they are hard pressed: when they cease to care about proprieties, and think only of the sore need of the moment. Such was the prayer of Peter, when he felt the waves yield beneath him—" Lord, save me ! I perish !" And as a mother will run when she hears her child scream, so God makes haste to respond to those cries of His children. To Him there are words in the cry. Its language is as intelligible as that of the priest supplicating at the altar. "Coming from our heart it reaches God's heart."

Thus much for the variety of prayer.

The second verse directs our thought to the *appropriating power* of prayer. God is addressed as *my* king; *my*

---

[1] Gurnall.

God. Our Lord's model of prayer strikes at all selfishness in our petitions. It bids us pray—" *Our* Father; Thy kingdom come to *us;* Give *us* bread; Forgive *us our* sins." At the same time, it does not exclude the personal element. No man is above the need of praying for himself; and God, in teaching us to pray, directs us to the many-sidedness of His character, and does not suffer us to forget, in our contemplation of His wonderful provision for the whole body of humanity, the equal wonder of His provision for the individual man, which gives him command of the whole ministry of heaven, as though he were alone in the universe. "These little pronouns—*my* king, *my* God, are," as has been justly observed, "the very pith and marrow of the plea. Here is an argument why God should answer prayer: because He is *our* king and *our* God. We are not aliens to Him. He is the king of our country. He is ours by covenant, ours by promise, ours by oath, ours by blood." [1]

By the third verse we are pointed to the *statedness* and *decency* of prayer. It is well that prayer should be spontaneous; but also well that it should be properly regulated. A rich soil is a good thing; but its richness is no reason why its fruits and grasses should be allowed to grow up in confusion. There are those who seem to think that any insistence on propriety in prayer implies heartless formalism. Not so our Psalm. In the first place, it suggests to us the propriety of *stated seasons* for prayer. "My voice shalt thou hear *in the morning.*" The gospel economy is indeed one of freedom and of spiritual man-

---

[1] Spurgeon.

hood; but, after all, we never get entirely beyond the necessity of rules. We are always the better for the adoption of some fixed lines of life; and as the temptations to negligence are nowhere more subtle and powerful than at our closet doors, it is well to fence these with a habit of prayer at a stated season. David indeed does not limit this to the morning. In the fifty-fifth Psalm he says: "Evening, morning, and at noon, will I pray and cry aloud." These seasons will vary in frequency and in time with the circumstances of individuals. The point to be insisted on is the having some season sacredly set apart for prayer, on which nothing shall be suffered to intrude. And what better season can be found than the morning? In the days of the old Roman empire, the gateways of rich and powerful citizens were thronged in the mornings with dependents, each bearing his basket, and waiting for the daily gift of food.[1] So it is fitting that our heavenly Father's gate should daily witness our presence, at the opening of the day, awaiting our share of the bread of heaven to nourish us for the day's responsibilities, trials, burdens, and temptations. And what is true of prayer regarded as petition, is equally true of prayer viewed as communion or as worship. It is fitting that the fresh energies of the morning, the clear, unwearied thought, the vigorous perception, the new enthusiasm, should be first called out towards Him. Then we are quicker to take His meaning, and calmer to face the coming issues of the day, and better disposed for that concentration of mind and heart which is indispensable to the effectiveness of prayer,

---

[1] Juvenal, Satire iii., 249.

"When first thy eyes unveil, give thy soul leave
    To do the like ; our bodies but forerun
The spirit's duty ; true hearts spread and heave
    Unto their God, as flowers do to the sun ;
Give Him thy first thoughts, then, so shalt thou keep
Him company all day, and in Him sleep.

Yet never sleep the sun up; prayer should
    Dawn with the day. There are set awful hours
'Twixt Heaven and us; the manna was not good
    After sun-rising, for day sullies flowers.
Rise to prevent the sun ; sleep doth sins glut,
And heaven's gate opens when the world's is shut.

Walk with thy fellow creatures; note the hush
    And whisperings amongst them. Not a spring
Or leaf but hath its morning hymn ; each bush
    And oak doth know I AM—canst thou not sing?
O leave thy cares and follies ! Go this way,
And thou art sure to prosper all the day." [1]

Note too the suggestion of decency in the act of prayer furnished by the word "*direct*." "In the morning will I direct my prayer to Thee." The original word is used of arranging the wood and the sacrifice upon the altar, which was one of the first duties of the priest as soon as day dawned,[2] and also of setting the loaves of the shew-bread in order upon the table. Thus the meaning is broader than that of our version, which conveys only the idea of *aiming* the prayer, as an arrow, in the right direction. It is rather—"I will pray, setting forth my supplication in order ; " or, as one puts it, "I will marshal my prayers. I will put them in order, and call up all my powers, and

---

[1] Henry Vaughan.   [2] Lev. vi. 12 ; Numb. xxviii. 4.

bid them stand in their proper places, that I may pray with all my might, and pray acceptably.'¹ In all this there is no suggestion which goes to make prayer unduly formal; nothing which tends to repress spontaneity or to fetter liberty. It merely teaches that prayer should be decorous and well pondered, and marked by an intelligent purpose. It strikes at the senseless bellowings and frenzied incoherencies, at the blasphemous familiarities with the name of God and with the work of Christ, which now and then appear in certain so-called acts of worship, perpetrated by those who ought to know better. It strikes equally at the hurried, perfunctory prayers of the man who goes into his closet without a previous thought of his needs, depending upon the moment for suggestions of the petitions he is to put up to God, and whose prayers, therefore, tend to run into a set of commonplaces and formal phrases, often carrying the most solemn and awful things, yet passing glibly from the tongue, only to be forgotten the moment the closet door lets him back to business or to pleasure. We should do well to cover less ground in our prayers, and to ponder their details more carefully. Take the familiar formulas of address, for instance : " Almighty God, our heavenly Father!" Stop just there. I am about to pray to the omnipotent and omniscient God, my Creator. My destinies and the world's are in His hands. My life hangs upon His will. He is my Father, too. Ah! you will wait long before you will have grasped all the wealth of goodness and of love conveyed in that single word—FATHER. One cannot thus weigh

---

[1] Trapp, quoted by Spurgeon.

his words without getting a new sense of the sacredness of prayer, and a growing dread of performing the duty hastily or thoughtlessly. And this, too, is a matter which affects our enjoyment of prayer. If it is your privilege to know a man of rich culture and of varied learning, you cannot enjoy these by running in each morning for a moment and exchanging a few inquiries about health, and a few commonplaces about the weather. Equally it is true that God cannot be enjoyed in hasty, perfunctory prayer. "He that believeth shall not make haste." [1]

This leads us naturally to a fourth characteristic of prayer—*expectancy*, suggested by the third verse—" I will watch or *look up*." As Elijah, when he had arranged the wood and the bullock on Carmel, looked up for the fire from Heaven, so he who has thoughtfully and reverently set forth his prayer before God, should expect the answer. He who prays otherwise mocks God; and yet how many pray as one who shoots an arrow at random, not looking to see what becomes of his shaft. What becomes of our prayers? Do we look to see whether they strike their mark or any mark? When a merchant counts his assets, he counts not only what he has in his storehouses, but what he has sent across the sea; and when we send forth these barques of prayer, laden with the dearest wishes and the deepest yearnings of our souls, is it nothing to us whether they arrive at their destined haven? "Never was faithful prayer lost at sea. No merchant trades with such certainty as the praying saint. Some prayers, indeed, have a longer voyage than others, but

---

[1] Isaiah xxviii. 16.

then they come with the richer lading at last. In trading, he gets most by his commodity that can do without his money longest. So the Christian that can with most patience stay for a return of prayer, shall never be ashamed of his waiting."[1] We are to *watch* and pray; to watch *unto* prayer—with reference to prayer; to watch *before* prayer, that our prayer may be rightly directed or set in order; to watch *during* prayer, against "unmannerly distractions;" to watch *after* prayer, to see what becomes of our prayers. Some one has very pithily said that the man who does not look after the prayers he has put up, is like the ostrich which lays her eggs and looks not for her young.

A fifth element of true prayer appears in the seventh verse:—*confidence;* that to which the apostle invites us when he says—"Let us therefore come boldly unto the throne of grace:"[2] The Psalmist speaks as one who has a right to come into God's house. It is his house because it is God's. The late Dr. Arnott, commenting on the words "They shall be abundantly satisfied with the fatness of Thy house," says—"I once heard a father tell that when he removed his family to a new residence where the accommodation was much more ample, the substance much more rich and varied than that to which they had previously been accustomed, his youngest son, yet a lisping infant, ran round every room and scanned every article with ecstasy, calling out, in childish wonder at every new sight, 'Is this *ours*, father? And is this *ours?*' The child did not say *yours;* and I observed that

---

[1] Gurnall.   [2] Hebrews iv. 16.

the father, while he told the story, was not offended with the freedom. You could read in his glistening eye that the infant's confidence in appropriating as his own all that his father had, was an important element in his satisfaction." What a beautiful comment this upon the apostle's words—"All things are yours, and ye are Christ's, and Christ is God's."[1] The child of God has no need to linger on his Father's threshold, nor to knock timidly. How differently a beggar and your child come to your office or study. The one raps hesitatingly, and awaits coweringly your permission to enter; while your boy bounds in at will, not always quietly, showing that he feels himself at home where his father is. The Christian has a child's place in God's house, and comes boldly to His mercy seat, and asks large things that his joy may be full.

Yet this confidence by no means excludes a sixth characteristic of prayer:—*humble reverence*. "As for me, I will come into Thy house, but I will come in the multitude of Thy mercy." It is of free grace, of undeserved compassion, of abounding love, that I am permitted to come. "Thou art not a God that hath pleasure in wickedness," and I am sinful. "The foolish shall not stand in Thy sight," and I have been the foolish prodigal who would have his portion, and who has wasted it in the far country. But Thou art *merciful;* and Thy mercy hath restored me, Thy pardon hath compassed Thy erring child about, Thou hast healed his backslidings and hast loved him freely; and so I come into Thy house,

---

[1] 1 Corinthians iii. 21, 23.

not because of my goodness or strength, but "in the multitude of Thy mercy," to pass the time of my sojourning in fear—godly, filial fear, as one whom thou hast redeemed at a price.[1]

And such an approach to God must involve the last element of prayer suggested by the Psalm—*joy:* "And all those who find refuge in Thee shall rejoice; forever shall they shout for joy." Why should they not? THOU defendest them. On earth, the intercourse of love is often marred by danger; but he who talks with God in His own house, always communes in safety. "He that dwelleth in the secret place of the Most High shall abide under the shadow of the Almighty."[2] Shall not God protect His own child in His own home? To talk familiarly with God, to come boldly into His house, to behold His beauty, to question Him freely, inquiring in His temple, to be safe in the shadow of His power, to be sure of His love and mercy, and solidly convinced of His infinite righteousness—well may such an one say, "Let them that love Thy name be joyful in Thee."

Thus this Psalm is a great lesson on prayer; pointing us to its variety as a weapon adapted for all emergencies, and teaching us how to wield it most effectively. We are taught to carry into it the faith which appropriates God as our own. We are warned against the profanation by carelessness or haste of that most solemn of acts—communion with our Creator. We are bidden to send forth our prayers considerately, and to look confidently for tidings from them. The Psalm drives all slavish fear

---

[1] 1 Peter i. 17, 18.   [2] Psalm xci. 1.

from our prayers even while it bases our confidence wholly upon the undeserved compassion of our Father in Heaven ; and it commends to us intercourse with God as no mere task or duty, but as the dearest employment and the sweetest joy of our lives.

THE PASTURE GATE.

PSALM XXIII.

(1) Jehovah is my Shepherd, I shall not want.
(2) In pastures of grass He maketh me to lie down;
Beside waters of rest doth He guide me.
(3) He restoreth my soul;
He leadeth me in the paths of righteousness,
For His name's sake.
(4) Yea, though I walk through the valley of the shadow of death,
I will fear no evil, for thou art with me:
Thy rod and thy staff—they comfort me.
(5) Thou preparest a table before me,
In the presence of mine enemies:
Thou hast anointed my head with oil.
My cup runneth over.
(6) Surely goodness and loving-kindness shall follow me all the days of my life,
And I will dwell in the house of Jehovah for length of days.

IV.

THE PASTURE GATE.

COMMON things do not give up their meaning to human reason, any more than a flint gives out sparks by contact with wood or clay. The word of God acts upon them as *steel* upon flint, and strikes divine fire out of them at every touch. How common and uninteresting an object is a shepherd, in his coarse garb, surrounded by his sheep; and yet the Spirit of God has made this figure one of the dearest and most suggestive images in the whole range of religious thought. The incarnate God Himself honored this name shepherd, by adopting it. Inspiration has brought out a vast range of analogies between the shepherd's functions and the attributes and ministries of the eternal Jehovah. How this Psalm has worked itself into the very texture of religious experience and of religious literature in all ages! To how many and how various phases of spiritual need it has ministered and continues to minister. It has a side for the poet, for the theologian, for the historian, for the antiquary, for the naturalist. Every variety of human sorrow flees to it as naturally as invalids to a healing spring. "The twenty-third Psalm is the nightingale of the Psalms. It is small, of a homely feather, singing shyly out of obscurity; but O, it has filled the air of the whole world with melodious joy greater than the heart can conceive. Blessed be the day on which that Psalm was born. What would you say of a pilgrim, commissioned by God to travel up and down the earth, singing a strange melody, which when one heard, caused him to forget whatever sorrow he had? Behold just such an one. This pilgrim God has sent to speak in every language on the globe. It has charmed more griefs to rest than all the philosophy of the world. It has remanded to their dungeon more felon thoughts, more black doubts, more thieving sorrows than there are sands on the sea-shore. It has comforted the noble host of the poor. It has sung courage to the army of the disappointed. It has poured balm and consolation into the heart of the sick, of captives in dungeons, of widows in their pinching griefs, of orphans in their loneliness. Nor is its work done. It will go singing to your children and my children through all the generations of time; nor will it fold its wings till the last pilgrim is safe and time ended; and then it shall fly back to the bosom of God whence it issued, and sound on, mingled with all those sounds of celestial joy which make heaven musical forever." [1]

No part of human experience is useless. We do indeed, as we become men, put away childish things, yet many of our childish experiences go farthest to mould manhood. We are prone to look upon our whole earlier life merely as a step by which we mount to something higher and better; yet we find, as we know ourselves better, that we have not left our first days entirely behind after all. David is an illustration of this fact. His life

---

[1] Henry Ward Beecher.

was a singularly varied one. He was shepherd, fugitive, court-favorite, minstrel, king, warrior—yet not one of these elements do we miss in the grand sum total of his character, viewed as a lesson to all ages and as a power of ministry to the Church. Least of all do we find wanting this shepherd experience of his youth. In the Psalms, more perhaps than in any other part of the Bible, the thoughts of God in nature, and of nature pointing up to God are emphasized; and David's utterances of this kind are largely the fruit of those early wanderings with his sheep, in green pastures, and by still waters, and through gloomy ravines, in the quick flashing bursts of the Eastern dawn, and under the gleam of the midnight stars. And if that shepherd life had furnished nothing else than the materials for this wonderful pastoral ode, we should all be inclined to say that no period of David's history would have compensated the Church for the loss of his shepherd life. Yet the Psalm is not the utterance of the shepherd days, though it perpetuates their memory. Had it been thus, men might have said that it was but the natural outflowing of a confiding boy's heart, unversed in care or struggle. But this peaceful idyl is a voice out of the maturer life of the Psalmist; out of memories of care and battle and treachery; a voice that tells that peace and rest of heart depend not upon the absence of life's burdens, nor on the presence of nature's tranquillizing scenes, but solely upon the shepherding of God.

The Psalm centres in this thought of God as a shepherd. All its ideas and images spring from this, and group themselves round it. Hence the key-note of the whole song is—GOD'S SERVANT FINDS HIS ALL IN GOD. He wants

nothing. All needs are met for him by that one fact—
The Lord is my shepherd. All prosperity is represented
to him by the fact that he is God's sheep in God's pastures,
led by God Himself. The problem of life is thus reduced
to its very simplest statement: the statement of Christ in
the home at Bethany—" But one thing is needful." [1] In
his prosperity, David might have said—" I have wealth, and
therefore I shall not want. I have faithful friends and brave
soldiers, and therefore I shall not want. I have reputation
and influence, and therefore I shall not want." And in saying this he would only have said what hundreds of men who
claim to be better instructed than David are saying to-day.
But David goes to the heart of the matter with the discern-
ment of the profoundest Christian philosopher; and in these
two brief sentences, sharply cuts out for us the eternal, vital
truth that man lives by God and not by His gifts; that
every good gift and every perfect gift is from above, from
the Father; and that the possession of all gifts is included
in possessing the Father.

This being true, it follows that the true end of every
man's life is to become one of God's flock. And here, the
figure, while it magnifies the wisdom and tenderness of
God, correspondingly depreciates the wisdom of man. To
represent man by a sheep, is to say that he is a weak, silly,
and defenceless creature, dependent for his well-being upon the care and protection of the shepherd. For a man
to seek to put himself under a shepherd's care, is for him
to admit this fact in all its length and breadth. The de-
pendence of man upon God must be just as absolute as that

---

[1] Luke x. 42.

of the sheep upon the shepherd. The guidance of the life cannot be shared between God and man, any more than between the shepherd and the sheep. Man is not to choose his own pastures, any more than the sheep are to choose theirs. Hence it is well for those who study and admire this Psalm for its poetry and for its sweet sentiments about God, to feel also the blow which it strikes at human pride and conceit. It is very charming, even for a worldly man, to contemplate this picture of the divine Shepherd by the peaceful streams; but such do not find it easy or pleasant to face the thought of taking the position of a sheep, with all that that position involves, even in those green pastures. Whether accidentally or not, this twenty-third Psalm immediately follows what has been called the Psalm of the cross—a prophetic description of the sufferings of Christ; and in the Christian application of the truth we have just alluded to, that is significant, as expressing the fact that man comes under the superintendence of the heavenly shepherd only by the way of the cross ; where, with Christ, his pride, and self-will, and self-righteousness are crucified, and he, like the humblest lamb in the flock, is made willing to follow the good Shepherd who gave his life for the sheep.

Yet, still carrying out the Christian application of the figure, there is a comforting assurance in the comparison of man to a sheep. For a sheep is not a wild animal. The lion and the bear are thrown upon their own resources; they wander far from the haunts of men; they are not brought to the markets, nor herded in pastures. The sheep, on the other hand, is associated with domestic scenes, the pet lamb is an inmate of the farm-yard, and the eye looks out from the cottage window, upon the pasture covered with flocks. A sheep is an object of purchase; and therefore an object of peculiar care, because he is *property;* and so, man, in accepting the position of a sheep, comes into a peculiarly close relation with God. He forfeits all power over himself, but he becomes God's own property; God's *valuable* property, since God shows the value He sets upon him by the price at which He buys him. Every redeemed soul in God's flock represents the blood of the only begotten Son of God; and this figure therefore is strictly in the line of the apostle Peter's thought —Peter, the apostle whom we should most naturally associate with this Psalm because of Christ's charge to him to feed His sheep and lambs—" Ye were not redeemed— bought back—with corruptible things, but with the precious blood of Christ, as of a lamb without blemish and without spot."[1] Shall one thus purchased want anything? "The young lions *do* lack and suffer hunger; but they that seek the Lord shall not want any good thing."[2] Shall the love which proved itself by the payment of such a price stop at any minor gift? "He that spared not His own Son but delivered Him up for us all, how shall He not with Him also freely give us all things?"[3]

And now, knowing thus generally that God's sheep shall not want, the Spirit leads us forth into the pastures to take note of some of the supplies.

And, first, our attention is called to the provision made for two sides of man's life in his new relation to God. A godly life, if it be healthful, must be both an active and a

---

[1] 1 Peter i. 18, 19.   [2] Psalm xxxiv. 10.   [3] Romans viii. 32.

contemplative life. In this age we are so constantly urged to active life that we are in some danger of losing sight of the claims of the contemplative life. While it is true that no life is more unhealthful and more fruitful in evil of some kinds than the life of the cloister—the life of pure contemplation as it is styled—it is equally true that the life of pure activity without contemplation is also unhealthful. If the one tends to paralysis, the other tends to fever. There are times when a man needs to lie still, like the earth under the spring rain, letting the lessons of experience and the memories of the word of God sink down to the very roots of his life, and fill the deep reservoirs of his soul. Those are not always lost days when his hands are not busy, any more than rainy days in summer are lost, because they keep the farmer in-doors. They are growing days; and for this side of the godly man's life the great Shepherd provides in His green pastures, He makes His servant to *lie down* there. There are times when men say they are too busy to stop; when they think they are doing God's service by going on. Now and then God *makes* such an one lie down. He has been driving through the pastures so fast that he has not known their greenness nor apprehended their sweet savor; and God does not mean that he shall lose all that, and so he makes him lie down: and then the active, bustling man learns the much-needed lesson of rest in the Lord, and of waiting patiently for Him, because he can do nothing else but rest; and when he once gets a little over his hurry and fretting, and begins to open his eyes to the greenness of the pastures, he finds that resting in God's pasture-lands is not such a bad thing after all. Many a man has had to thank God for some such enforced season of rest, in which he first learned the sweetness of meditation on the Word, and of lying still in God's hands and waiting God's pleasure.

At the same time, the Shepherd provides for the active side of the life. There is motion under God's leadership. "He *leadeth* me beside the still waters." The fact that activity is an essential element of a godly life, is too familiar to need comment; but we may observe how it is possible for some of the calmness and tranquillity of the contemplative life to perpetuate itself in the active life. There are indeed times when one stops beside the flowing stream, and leisurely surveys its beauties or disports himself in its waters; but even as he goes on, he may keep the stream in sight, and be soothed by its soft ripple, and refreshed by its varied scenery. And just so it is possible for a man to make his active life restful. He may carry the atmosphere of the closet into the street. There is no contradiction in this. The Shepherd promises to lead him beside still waters; and those are the deepest waters. Christ Himself says "I will give you rest," even while He says in the same breath, "Take My yoke upon you." [1] This feverish, hurried life which too many of us lead, is not in God's economy, depend upon it. If we live in this way, it is because we push on *before* the Shepherd, instead of letting him *lead* us beside still waters. If we were more docile, we should be more restful.

Only when the soul is brimful of the life of faith does it work in rest. Not until we shall have let our life drop back behind God, to follow at the rate which He pre-

---

[1] Matthew xi. 28, 29.

scribes, shall we learn what the words mean—"Thou wilt keep him in perfect peace whose mind is stayed on Thee."[1]

Our errors in this and in other things, point us to a farther need for which we find provision made as we go on with the Psalm;—RESTORATION; "He restoreth my soul." Eastern travellers tell us that the shepherd is much occupied with the *straying* sheep. Only a few keep near him. The majority run from bush to bush, jump into neighboring fields, climb into leaning trees from which they fall and break their limbs, or wander to great distances and get lost among the mountain defiles; so that much of the shepherd's time and care are consumed in seeking and restoring these wanderers. Similarly, it is true, that restoration occupies a prominent place in God's economy; indeed it is *essentially* an economy of restoration. Here we see restoration under three phases; 1st—forgiveness. It is not too much to say that the whole human flock is made up of straying sheep. Even while we sing: "We are His people and the sheep of His pasture,"[2] we must needs run into the minor strain —"Have mercy upon me, O God, according to Thy loving-kindness. Wash me thoroughly from mine iniquity, and cleanse me from my sin."[3] It is here that the shepherdly tenderness of God pre-eminently appears:—just here where the world's shallow charity exhausts itself. The world will yield to almost any prayer sooner than to the prayer for forgiveness. David might well ask to fall into God's hands rather than into man's; for it is

---

[1] Isaiah xxvi. 3.   [2] Psalm c. 3.   [3] Psalm li. 1, 2.

man's way to say "Let the foolish, headstrong, conceited sheep reap the reward of its folly." But hear how Psalm and Gospel answer to each other. "He restoreth my soul." "How think ye? If a man have a hundred sheep, and one of them be gone astray, doth he not leave the ninety and nine and goeth into the mountains, and seeketh that which is gone astray? And if so be that he find it, verily I say unto you, he rejoiceth more of that sheep than of the ninety and nine which went not astray. Even so it is not the will of your Father which is in Heaven that one of these little ones should perish." [1]

Then too, this restoration appears in the rest and refreshment bestowed upon faithful servants. Good men become weary, not *of* doing God's will, but *in* doing it. Even Jesus, whose meat was to do the will of Him that sent Him, was faint at Jacob's well. How many ways God has of refreshing the courage and toning up the enthusiasm of His weary ones:—now by a promise, now by a well-timed success, now by a lightening of the burden. What, for example, is the Sabbath but one of those green pastures, fenced round by a divine mandate— "In it thou shalt do no work." How often the Lord repeats to His later disciples the invitation to the twelve— "Come ye yourselves apart into a desert place and rest awhile." [2] You remember how the pilgrims in Bunyan's allegory went on their way to a pleasant river, upon the banks of which they "walked with great delight; they drank also of the water of the river which was pleasant and enlivening to their weary spirits. On either side of

---

[1] Matthew xviii. 12, 14. [2] Mark vi. 31.

the river was also a meadow, curiously beautified with lilies; and it was green all the year long. In this meadow they lay down and slept, for here they might *lie down safely*. When they awoke they gathered again of the fruit of the trees, and drank again of the water of the river, and then lay down again to sleep. Thus they did several days and nights. Then they sang:

> Behold ye how these crystal streams do glide,
> To comfort pilgrims by the highway side;
> The meadows green, beside their fragrant smell,
> Yield dainties for them: and he that can tell
> What pleasant fruit, yea leaves, these trees do yield,
> Will soon sell all, that he may buy this field."

Again, this restorative care comes in where all care but the Shepherd's is valueless;—in times of sorrow. No touch then is so tender as that of the very staff which smites. And of all these phases of restoration it is to be observed that they are *radical:* they act upon the springs of the life. "He restoreth my *soul—*my *life.*" Is it forgiveness? He puts "a new heart" into man. Is it refreshment? Its fountain-head is rest of heart. Is it consolation? His words go deeper than the cold conventionalities of men; they bring the abiding peace of settled trust in fatherly love, and of the vision of eternal joy.

And the thought which follows is kindred to this restorative economy of God. "He leadeth me in the paths of righteousness for His name's sake." The ways of *righteousness* or *rightness*. God seeks to make His children right for their own good, but primarily for His glory; for their highest good is involved in His being glorified. "Seeing He hath taken upon Him the name of a good Shepherd, He will discharge His part, whatever His sheep be. It is not their being *bad* sheep that can make Him leave being a *good* shepherd, but He will be good and maintain the credit of His name in spite of all their badness; and though no benefit come to them of it, yet there shall glory accrue to Him by it, and His name shall nevertheless be magnified and extolled."[1] In the man once restored, God shows forth His own righteousness. He makes him a partaker of the divine nature. He does more than bring him back to the fold; his restoration is only the beginning of the divine manhood in him. Nor does God set Himself to develop some single virtue merely. He leads him not in one path, but in *paths* of righteousness. The new character permeates the man's whole being and all this is for HIS 'NAME'S sake; not for man's glory:.O, no! What has man had to do with the matter? All his part has been, like a wounded sheep, to lie still in the Shepherd's strong arms, and be carried back to the safe and peaceful fold. All his part henceforth is to follow in the paths where God shall lead him. It is for His name's sake; "that in the ages to come he might show the exceeding riches of His grace in his kindness towards us through Christ Jesus."[2] It is to vindicate His promise that He will make a grand, pure, efficient manhood out of this wreck of character. It is to show how His grace can make a blazing beacon out of a charred brand, a mitred priest out of a criminal.[3] How

---

[1] Sir Richard Baker.   [2] Ephesians ii. 7.   [3] Zechariah iii. 2, 5.

His wisdom can preserve him in temptation, how His power can keep him from falling, and present him blameless at last before His presence. "For Mine own sake, even for Mine own sake will I do it; for how should My name be polluted? And I will not give my glory to another."[1]

With the fourth verse, we pass into another scene. The recollections of the natural scenery amid which David fed his sheep, give coloring to the Psalm and shape its imagery. Often his wanderings had brought him to one of those gloomy ravines which penetrate the cliffs overhanging the Dead Sea: places beset with dangers; for here the robber made his haunt, and the beast of prey lurked. In the figurative meaning of these words, the Psalmist's reference was not primarily to death. A "valley of death" or of "death-darkness," was simply a very dark and gloomy valley; but the Church in all ages has delighted to find, as it rightfully may, an allusion to the last and sorest strait of the believer—the agony of death; and these words have been quoted by more dying lips than any ten texts of Scripture together. We need not therefore try to divert the thought from this familiar channel. Here where he most needs Him, God's child finds the shepherd with His rod and staff. Let us look at the verse a little in detail. "Yea, though I *walk*." It is perhaps a little fanciful, yet it is a beautiful and comforting fancy which a modern preacher[2] has drawn out of the English text:—"Yea, though I *walk*. As if the believer did not quicken his pace when he came to die, but still calmly walked with

---

[1] Isaiah xlviii. 11.   [2] Spurgeon.

God. To walk indicates the steady advance of a soul which knows its road, knows its end, resolves to follow the path, feels quite safe, and is therefore perfectly calm and composed. The dying saint is not in a flurry. He does not run as if he were alarmed, nor stand still as though he would go no farther; he is not confounded nor ashamed, and therefore keeps his old place." Thus Enoch walked with God; and our last glimpse of him reveals him still walking in the same blessed company, as God gently takes him out at the gate which leads to heaven.

Then look at the word *shadow :*—"the shadow of death." Literally it means only the darkness or shade: and yet there is a Gospel thought in the word. Suppose your child, walking with you, should come to the mouth of a ravine, and should see cast across it the gigantic shadow of an armed man, at which he should begin to cry and draw back in terror. And suppose that you should take him not into the shadow, but around behind the armed man, and show how he was chained fast to his post, and could not move a step toward the road, nor hurl a dart at a traveller. And is not this just what the Gospel does for us poor children of dust?

> "We start and fear to die:
> What timorous worms we mortals are!"

Our hearts grow cold as we approach the entrance to the valley, and we see the shadow of gigantic arms and of pointed darts before us in the pathway; but our blessed Shepherd comes to meet us. He sits down with us there at the mouth of the valley, and tells us of His fight with

The Pasture Gate. 67

the monster. He tells us that He "abolished death;"[1] that through death He destroyed "him that had the power of death," that He might "deliver them who through fear of death were all their lifetime subject to bondage."[2] He shows His child that the monster is chained: that he has not to encounter the dart, but only to pass through the shadow: and with this assurance, the "Feeble-minds" and "Ready-to-halts" rise and strike boldly into the darkness, and we hear them saying as they pass from our sight— "O death, where is thy sting? O grave, where is thy victory?"[3]

Nor does the Shepherd merely tell the story of His own victory. He does not leave His follower to go through the valley alone. "Thou art with me: Thy rod and Thy staff they comfort me." The shepherd carries with him a rod or crook to guide the flock and to correct them when they are disobedient, and a staff on which to lean. Both these—His rod and His staff the divine Shepherd offers to His people to comfort them therewith; and we must not miss the force of that good old word "comfort." It means far more than simply to console. It signifies to tone up the whole nature, to *strengthen* a man so that all his energy can be brought to bear. If anywhere he needs comfort in this sense, it is in the valley of the shadow; and so God comforts him first with His *rod*, the instrument of correction. Aye, *comforts* him with the *rod:* for the very afflictions and pains which wait about the entrance to the valley are God's messengers and instruments of perfection to make him meet for a better inheritance. Do

---

[1] 2 Timothy i. 10.   [2] Hebrews ii. 14.   [3] 1 Corinthians xv. 55.

you remember those words of God to Israel by the prophet Ezekiel? "I will cause you to pass under the rod, and I will bring you into the bond of the covenant;"[1] and do you know the picture that was in the prophet's mind? He had stood by one of those stone enclosures where the sheep are folded for the night, and he had seen the shepherd stand by the door as the sheep passed in, laying his rod across the entrance that they might not crowd in so rapidly as to prevent his counting them. Every sheep passes under the rod before it enters the fold; and so the shepherd gets none but his own and all of his own. So stands the great Shepherd before the eternal gate, and every one of His chosen shall pass under the rod,—the rod which sometimes smites and bruises, that, being made perfect through suffering, they may be counted among them that are sanctified. And then, when the rod has done its work, the staff is given. When the pilgrim's knees begin to totter, then come "the everlasting arms,"[2] and the strong staff makes firm his step, and naught can shake his foothold until he passes out of the shadow into the light of heaven.

The fifth verse develops a new and interesting line of thought in setting forth the relations of God's child to those outside the fold; whereas the Psalm thus far has been occupied with his relations to the Shepherd. It is enough to say that the relation to the Shepherd settles every minor relation. The very enemies of God are compelled to acknowledge the prosperity of His child. They cannot molest him. They frown impotently upon him as

---

[1] Ezekiel xx. 37.   [2] Deuteronomy xxxiii. 27.

the robber might have looked down upon the sheep feeding in the pastures, without the power of annoying them. He is without fear in their very presence. He has not even to snatch his meal hurriedly; a table is deliberately spread while they look on, and the anointing, and the overflowing cup which mark the ceremonious welcome of a guest, are bestowed in the presence of his foes. Even so does God's child feast on angels' food, while cares eddy round him, and temptations beset, and slander wags its tongue, and sickness and pain and misfortune thrust sore at him. Why should he not rest and feast? The Lord is his shepherd.

"Perhaps," says a recent expositor of the Psalms,[1] "there is no Psalm in which the absence of all doubt, misgiving, fear, anxiety, is so remarkable." It might be added that the sense of trustfulness becomes more positive as the Psalm proceeds, until, in the last verse, it culminates in an exultant outburst of assurance as respects the writer's future lot. The future is no less secure than the present. "Surely goodness and mercy shall follow me all the days of my life." And note that the basis of this assurance is not the fact that God has allotted him his place in green pastures, but in the fact that the Lord is his Shepherd. He clearly perceives that it may be God's pleasure to change this happy lot and to direct his course into the gloomy valley of the shadow; but the goodness and the loving kindness shall none the less be his. Goodness and mercy do not mean to God's child flowering meads and wells of refreshment only; they may equally mean rocky defiles,

---

[1] Canon Perowne.

and rough paths, and darkness, and enemies. When Paul promises the Corinthians all things in Christ, he couples, in the most natural and matter-of-course way, death and things to come, with life and things present, treating them all alike as God's good gifts.[1] It is all one so long as they are Christ's. Goodness and loving kindness, now and evermore, are represented to David simply by those five words—THE LORD IS MY SHEPHERD. Darkness, roughness, hostility, will be goodness and mercy still, so long as they shall not separate him from his Shepherd's society, guidance and comfort. There are dark rooms in God's own house, in which He appoints that His children dwell sometimes. It matters little so long as they are under His roof. "ONE THING," says David, elsewhere, "have I desired of the Lord: *that* will I seek after."[2] Not sunshiny days: the Lord is my light. Not earthly security: the Lord is my salvation. Not human strength: the Lord is the strength of my life. I need not the beauties of art or of nature, if I may behold the beauty of Jehovah. I can dispense with human wisdom, if I may inquire in His temple. "One thing have I desired of the Lord— that I may dwell in the house of the Lord all the days of my life."

I know not whether David's thought reached beyond this life. "To him it may have been enough that he was the sheep for whom the Divine Shepherd cared, the guest for whom the Divine Host provided."[3] Yet he may, on the other hand, have seen farther than we think. It may be that, in the words of Calvin, "he shows in this passage

---

[1] 1 Corinthians iii. 21–23.   [2] Psalm xxvii. 4.   [3] Perowne.

that he lives least of all in earthly pleasures and profits, but sets a mark for himself in heaven to which he refers all things." Be that as it may, in the light of Christ's words concerning Himself as the Good Shepherd, David's words speak to the Christian reader of heaven no less than of earth. This psalm and the tenth chapter of John form two links in a chain which finds its completing link in the seventh chapter of Revelation—" Therefore are they before the throne of God, and serve Him day and night in His temple, and He that sitteth on the throne shall spread His habitation over them.[1] They shall hunger no more, neither thirst any more, neither shall the sun ever light upon them, no, nor any heat; because the LAMB, which is in the midst of the throne, SHALL SHEPHERD THEM, and shall guide them to the fountains of the waters of life; and God shall wipe away every tear out of their eyes."

---

[1] Or, more literally, " shall *pavilion* them."

THE REGISTRY GATE

4

PSALM XXV.

7. Remember not the sins of my youth, nor my transgressions. According to Thy mercy remember Thou me for Thy goodness' sake, O Lord.

V.

THE REGISTRY GATE.

THE true significance of the present is not revealed in the present. The present usually tells us only half truths, and sometimes falsehoods. Time detaches our actions from the circumstances which color them, from the unconscious influences which give them bias, and leaves them before us in their naked good or evil. Only the lapse of years makes us dispassionate judges of our earlier selves.

And hence the past often, perhaps commonly, comes into our maturer life as an element of pain and reproach. There is not one of us who has not said, again and again—"What would I not give to have this or that thing to do over again with to-day's experience. How much better I would do it. How differently I would plan it. How many things I would omit from it."

This text is such an expression. It is the utterance of a ripe and rich experience—of a man about whom the shadows have begun to lengthen, and who is letting a sorrowful and faultful past come home to his matured judgment, to be tried by its higher standards and by its clearer discrimination.

And yet, with the knowledge we have of David's youth,

we are, at first, astonished at the keenness of feeling manifest in this prayer. So far as we know, his youth and early manhood were comparatively innocent. He had led the life of a simple shepherd, he had not been spoiled by parental indulgence, but had rather been the servant of a family of older brothers. That he had shown real courage, and fidelity, and piety, while yet an underling, his history bears witness. That he had meditated on the glory of God in nature appears from the inspired songs of his later life. That he had undergone the discipline of sorrow and persecution before the world's burden comes heavily on most men—we can see for ourselves. Why then does he so earnestly plead that the sins of his youth be not remembered by God?

The answer to this question is to be found in the standpoint from which David contemplated his life; for while the cool retrospect of a life brings disappointment and disgust to every thoughtful man, the nature and degree of this disgust are regulated according to the standard of judgment which is applied. The majority of men come, sooner or later, to think of themselves as *fools* in their earlier years, but they do not likewise come to think of themselves as *sinners*. One may look back upon the errors of his earlier life with an amused chagrin, coupled with an easy tolerance, as he would view to-day the follies of a child. He may lament over many a sinful deed, not because of its sinfulness, but because he now sees how it affected his self-interest, impaired his health or his fortune, or made him a laughing-stock where he desired to shine. If he has a warning for another, it is not based on the *moral obliquity* of his course, but on its disadvantages.

He sees a youth indulging in drink or in licentiousness, and he says—"It will not *pay*. Look at me and take warning lest you be diseased or crippled as I am." He does not call on God not to remember his errors, but tries to forget them himself, and is quite content if he can bring himself to believe that they have not impaired his social standing, nor put farther pleasure out of his power.

And with such views, one's retrospect is, naturally, very limited and partial. His rule of judgment is short, and is laid off in wide spaces. It measures only grosser errors, or those which entail direct consequences. Much which went to give the most decisive bent and shape to character, is entirely overlooked.

But when one begins to review his life from the standpoint of his moral relation to God, he sees through a glass which greatly enlarges the range of his retrospect. Thoughts as well as deeds, intention as well as performance, motive no less than act—enter into his review. Secret faults come under inspection with presumptuous sins: what he is not, as well as what he is. His losses are tried by another standard. The result of years of honest toil, his full storehouses, his praises on the lips of men, may seem as nothing beside the possible moral achievements in which he has failed.

Thus it is with David. He hints at a page of his earlier history which he does not turn for us. There have been other wanderings in his youth than those beside still waters, concerning which he communes only with God and with his own heart; and whatever his youthful days may seem to others, they come back to him laden with experiences upon which, if it were possible, he would shut even the memory of God. "Remember not the sins of my youth."

But why does David plead so earnestly for this?—for this Psalm is the cry of a man in trouble, and burdened with painful apprehensions. The truth assumed in these words is one which concerns the character of God, which gives tone to this whole prayer of David, and which it very much concerns us to see as clearly as he did—the truth, namely, that God cannot be *passive* in any moral relation. If God's remembrance (humanly speaking) of sin began and ended with itself, if David's sins or your sins or mine were merely stored up in the Divine mind as an insignificant fact or date is retained in our minds, David had no need to trouble himself, nor have we. But sin cannot come to the notice of God without setting something in motion against itself, any more than the poles of a battery can be brought together without starting an electric current. An infinitely and essentially holy Nature cannot be aware of sin, without being roused to active dealing with it. He could not be passive toward it and remain true to himself. It is aimed at the pillars of His throne, it is a challenge of His sovereignty, a departure from His established order. He must rouse himself either to thwart it, or to punish it, or to turn it, spite of itself, to some beneficent end, or to forgive it. He cannot let it alone. As a Lawgiver, he must take cognizance of violated law. As a Father, he must strive to restore an erring son. As an administrator, he must anticipate the far-reaching consequences of a violation of moral order. For God to remember sin is to assume an active and hostile relation to sin. When the sins of men rise to His presence, like the sun-drawn drops to the upper air, the clouds gather and the thunders mutter.

Here is where men make such a vital mistake. They are deceived, and mock God by thinking that He can, by any possibility, be false to His own pure being. They measure Him by their own standards, and think that their own good-natured tolerance of sin is mirrored in Him. You may take a piece of common window-glass and put it in the photographer's camera, and let the sunbeams stream through the lens upon it for a week, and it will be as blank at the end of that time as when you put it in. Put the coated plate in its place for a second, and the smallest object is reproduced with a fidelity which bears the test of the microscope. Perhaps, if the window-glass were conscious, it might wonder at the sensitiveness of the prepared plate, just as men wonder and chafe when they are told of the sensitiveness of Divine purity to the slightest development of evil. "Why repel us," they say, "with the picture of so strict a God? Why should He make so much of what we generously tolerate in each other?" Simply because His nature is not like yours. You think Him altogether such an one as yourself. You transfer to Him your own obtuseness. You do not see that God's nature must, by the law of its own perfection, recoil from evil ; that He must rouse himself to extirpate it from a universe into which it is an intruder; that truth must array itself actively against the smallest falsehood, and purity against the faintest shadow of a stain. Thus this thought of God remembering sin, is a pregnant thought. It means, not a dry inventory in the Divine mind, but a stirring up of the Divine indignation; a setting in motion of the recording angel's pen, writing down to the sinner's credit his lawful wages—*death*. Well might David pray —" remember not the sins of my youth."

And if we stop here, the case is sad enough; but David, while he prays like a man in anguish, prays also like a man in hope, with an assurance that something may yet be done with those iniquities stored up in the memory of God, so that they shall cease to trouble or to threaten him any more. Being confronted with this startling problem, he applies directly to the only person who can solve it—to Him against whom he has sinned.

If a man will once deliberately consider the outbranchings and consequences of a single sin, even in the light of familiar laws of cause and effect, he will readily see what a stupendous problem is that of forgiveness, and will echo the scribe's question—" Who can forgive sins but God only?"[1] For take any single sinful act, such as the carelessness and wantonness of youth often perpetrate, and see how it goes on multiplying itself, setting in motion evil forces which, in their turn, set others in motion, drawing ever new victims into the train of consequences, unaffected, in all physical results, by prayers and tears—and who is bold enough to so much as attempt to trace out and remedy the woe that has sprung up along its lines? And when the ramifications of a whole life of sin are contemplated, with all their multiplied crossing and recrossing consequences—as well attempt to reduce to order a tropical jungle. It cannot be done.

---

[1] Mark ii. 7.

The most ordinary mind at once discerns the impossibility of retrieving and correcting the results of a sinful life. They are beyond the reach of money, time, and labor. The only course possible is to put the whole tangled mass into God's hands. This David at once perceives, and to this end he prays—"Unto thee, O Lord do I lift up my soul. I know not how the gigantic, hopeless task is to be performed, but I throw it upon Thy wisdom. Mine eyes are ever towards the Lord, for He shall pluck my feet out of the net."

And now, what are we to expect in answer to such an appeal as this?

Certainly not that God will literally shut these things out of His remembrance. This, it need hardly be said, is essentially impossible. "All things are," and must continue to be, "naked and open unto the eyes of Him with whom we have to do."[1]

Nor yet are we to expect that God will change His attitude toward sin. That is unalterably fixed. So long as He is God, He can have but one feeling towards sin of every kind and degree—utter loathing.

But while God's relation to sin remains fixed as the principles of His own being, His relation with the *sinner* may be changed. As we have seen that His remembrance of sin involves active hostility to sin, so we may now see that His remembrance of the sinner involves all the infinite activity of His love towards the sinner. " God commendeth His love toward us in that while we were yet *sinners* Christ died for us."[2] The prodigal's father loved

---

[1] Hebrews iv. 13. [2] Romans v. 8.

him no less when he sat among the swine, than when he had him at his table with the ring on his hand. It was the son's love and not the father's that had wandered. And, such being the case, we may expect that when a man is put in right relation to this unchanging love of God, that love will put him in some new relation to his old sins which will suffer them no longer to come between God and His child, and which will be, to all intents and purposes, as though God had literally *forgotten* them.

It is on this relation of God to the sinner that David throws himself. When he looks at the sins of his youth, he prays—"O Lord, forget them." When he looks at himself, he cries—"O Lord, remember me according to Thy mercy. Not according to my efforts at reformation, not according to the depth of my sorrow, not according to my attempts at restitution, but according to Thy mercy remember Thou me for Thy goodness' sake, O Lord. I know that Thou frownest on the rampant passion of youth: remember it not, O Lord; but I know that Thou dost pity the weak and passion-blinded youth. Such was I. Remember *me*, O Lord. I know that Thou hatest self-conceit. Remember not my foolish vanity. But I know Thy fatherly heart yearns over the straying son, who, in his self-sufficiency, flees from Thy wise and tender guidance. So did I. Remember me, O Lord, for Thy goodness' sake, not toward sin, but towards Thine erring children whose frame Thou knowest and rememberest that they are dust."[1]

---

[1] Psalm ciii. 14.

How then, in answer to this prayer, will man stand related to the follies and sins of his past life?

He will not be entirely rid of their consequences, especially of their *physical* consequences. If a youth of dissipation has undermined his health, God will not work a miracle and make him sound again. If a youth of indolence has made him the inferior of men of his own years in knowledge, culture, or disciplined power, the loss will not be fully made up.

Nor will God cease to use the faultful past in the new man's education. He will point His new lessons with the warnings which the old experience has burnt deep into His pupil's memory. He will keep him back from many an enchanted ground by the bitter remembrance of old bondage; and He will touch his lips with the eloquence of sad experience, as He shall use him to warn others from the way whose end is death.

He will never taunt him with the past. He wants to use the past as a help only, not as a sting. See how Jesus dealt with Peter,—Peter the braggart, the swearer, the coward, the denier of his Lord. Christ had plainly foretold it all to Peter, and yet, when the third denial fell from his lips, He did not turn upon him and say—"I told you so." He only looked at him and broke His heart. And then, on that memorable morning by the lake,[1] after the resurrection, what an opportunity for holding Peter up to the ridicule of his companions, or for recalling his treachery with scathing words: and yet the only hint of the sorrowful past was conveyed in the question—"Lovest

---

[1] John xxi.

thou Me more than these?" As if He had said—"Have you learned your severe lesson, or are you still the same Peter who professed such surpassing love for Me?"

And into the heart there will come a tranquil rest, a deep peace, founded not upon hope of retrieving the past, for there may be little time left; but simply upon the conviction that God has taken the whole sadly confused and stained life into His own hands. Even while the man looks upon the

> "Confusions of a wasted youth,"

and perhaps of a wasted manhood, he realizes that the strain has passed over from him to Christ. Often one keeps fighting in a helpless sort of way, not because he has any real hope of making good the past, but because he is conscientiously afraid to drop all concern about it: and there is blessed relief in giving over the struggle; in accepting the conclusion that it *is* hopeless, and that, if the consequences of past sin are to be adjusted at all, God must do it in His own time and way.

And with this conclusion there will come a turning with fresh zest to redeem the time which remains. God says to him: "Forget the things that are behind, even though the most of your life is behind. In the little time that remains, throw off the burden of the past on Me and press forward."

> "Old age hath yet his honor and his toil;
> Death closes all: but something ere the end,
> Some work of noble note may yet be done.

The wise woman of Tekoah gave David good advice

when she bade him cease mourning for the slain Amnon, and call home the banished Absalom. "We must needs die," she said, "and are as water spilt on the ground, which cannot be gathered up again ; neither doth God respect any person ; yet doth He devise means that His banished be not expelled from Him."[1] Yes, we must needs die. Our dying, weak natures, unstable as water, have proved their quality in the abuse of past years ; yet God, for that reason, will not cut off the opportunities that remain. He forbids you to seek the living among the dead. He tells you not to pass the days that are left in mourning over what is dead, but to spend them in coming back from your banishment, through the faithful use of the means which His infinite grace has devised.

Hither then we bring the past. Into these skilful hands we may put the hopelessly entangled mesh, wet with penitent tears, and turn our faces peacefully and firmly to the future, as we hear our justly offended but still loving Father saying : " I will be merciful to their unrighteousness, and their sins and their iniquities will I remember no more."[2] God only can adjust the past. Whether you know and believe it or not, the element of bitterness in it, the thing which makes it a burden, is sin ; and for sin there is but one remedy. That which has made all other relations ineffective or disastrous, has been the want of a proper relation to God. The great thing now, the immediate, pressing duty, is to get into a right relation with Him.

Look forward therefore. Hear the apostle responding

---

[1] 2 Samuel xiv. 14.   [2] Hebrews viii. 12.

to the son of Jesse: "Forgetting those things which are behind, and reaching forth unto those things which are before, I press toward the mark for the prize of the high calling of God in Christ Jesus."[1] The *high* calling. Yes, God is calling us from the low ground of tears, from the heavy atmosphere of sighs, from a dead past, up to the high table-lands of a present full of work and of aspiration. We have made mistakes: then let us remember that, in the stirring words of Robertson, "Life, like war, is a series of mistakes; and he is not the best Christian nor the best general who makes the fewest false steps. Poor mediocrity may secure that; but he is the best who wins the most splendid victories by the retrieval of mistakes. Forget mistakes. Organize victory out of mistakes."

You are not what you desire to be; not what you ought to be. But why look back? If God is ready to forget the sins of your youth, why may not you leave them behind also? If there is any good in store for you, it lies on before.

Granting your attainments were ever so great, *they* would not win you the prize. If you shall ever be admitted to the Lamb's marriage feast, it will be in borrowed robes, in Christ's righteousness, not in yours. You can do but one thing, look unto Jesus and go forward.

One may be sadly saying to-day, "It is too late. My cheek is furrowed, my hair is white, the days of my strength are gone, and they have been given, not to God, but to the world. I have but a few withered stalks to bring to the Lord of the harvest." Well, it *is* sad, but

---

[1] Philippians iii. 13, 14.

then it is done. You cannot bring back past time now, and for the time which remains, which is the better course—to stay in that old past, rummaging amid its broken plans and distorted forms for a little comfort and self-gratulation, or to leave it all in the hands of a tender, pitying Christ, and to let Him send you forth to the vineyard at the eleventh hour? Surely the latter is the better course. Begin to press forward, and it may yet be with you as sometimes, after a day of dark clouds, and howling wind, and driving rain, just at eventide the veil lifts itself from the gloomy west, and the sun goes down in a glory of purple and gold, which sets the dark pines on fire, and bathes the frowning rocks with splendor. Jesus can fill these later hours, free from the heat of youthful passion and of wild ambition, with tranquil hope, with holy joy, aye, and with some good work which may yet leave the world the richer for your having lived.

THE TREASURY GATE.

PSALM XXXI.

(19.) Oh how great is Thy goodness, which thou hast laid up for them that fear Thee ; which Thou hast wrought for them that trust in Thee before the sons of men.

VI.

THE TREASURY GATE.

WHEN a man searching for metals lights upon a fragment of gold or copper or iron ore, he is apt to conclude that the fragment is part of a larger mass—a metallic vein. The same is true of the words of Scripture. We find everywhere single verses which sparkle with truth, single words heavy with Divine meaning; but closer examination shows that they belong to great *veins* of truth, and lie in the line of *great principles* of God's administration. This text, for instance, is the expression of a divine *law :* the law of *God's wise reserve in dispensing His favors.* He does not reveal Himself, nor bestow His blessings, nor develop His purposes, nor mature His plans all at once. This latter is what an ignorant and vulgar conception of God would demand. To some minds the highest ideal of God would be a magician, after the pattern of Aladdin's genius, who should gratify every monstrous wish for the asking, and accomplish, with a touch, the results of years of human labor.

The God of Scripture is not such as this. Whether in nature or in providence, we see God revealing Himself through processes. In the revolution of the year, we see a progress of the seasons from the cold and apparent deadness of winter, to the rich fruitfulness laid up in the heart of the autumn. Man advances to the inheritance of the powers and enjoyments of manhood by slow gradations, from a feebleness and helplessness compared with which the infancy of a dog or of a horse is robust vigor. God's great plans in the administration of the world consume centuries. Christ did not come until the fulness of time had arrived; and Christ himself illustrated the growth of God's kingdom in the world by the slow processes of vegetation. Thus, at each season of the year, at each human birthday, at each stage of the world's history, there is something still in reserve; something *laid up;* something which God holds back because the time is not ripe.

Here we have a single application of this principle to our personal experience of God's goodness. "How great is Thy goodness which Thou hast *laid up* for them that fear Thee." The words "*laid up*" literally mean "*hidden;*" and the verse may be construed in two senses, which, however, often blend in one thought. The first sense is—that God's best gifts are *peculiarly* the treasure of those who fear Him. They are laid up or hidden from the rest of the world, just as a rich father lays up a fortune for his child and for him only. They are as a *secret* between God and his child; as the Psalmist elsewhere says—"The secret of the Lord is with them that fear Him."[1] It was this side of the thought which Christ expressed when he said, "I have meat to eat which ye know not of"[2]—and which is also conveyed in the promise, "To him that overcometh will I give to eat of the *hidden* manna."[3]

---

[1] Psalm xxv. 14.   [2] John iv. 32.   [3] Revelation ii. 17.

The Treasury Gate. 93

The other sense is in the line of the general principle we have illustrated; namely, that in the distribution of His blessings to His children, God follows a law of *reserve*. He gives liberally, but not the whole. He keeps something always in the background; there is always something better in store for those who fear Him. There is in His word, His promises, His providences a hidden element which comes out only through time, and experience, and search, and diligent effort.

The case cannot be otherwise. Reverently speaking, according to the laws which God Himself has stamped upon our being, He cannot deal otherwise with us. There are certain great blessings of God which no man is able to receive at once, without preparation. In respect of this, the law is not different in the spiritual region from the law in ordinary life. There are, for instance, great treasures, rich enjoyments, grand powers laid up for the schoolboy in the realm of knowledge and culture upon which he is just entering; but his teacher cannot put him in possession of them at once. He must gain the preparatory discipline first; the rudimentary knowledge without which all that lies beyond would be useless. So the judicious executor has a rich fortune in store for his ward; but he cannot, with safety to the child, put him in possession of his fortune without ruining both him and the fortune. He must be prepared by education and by contact with the world to administer his affairs before he can enjoy his wealth. God had a wonderful work to do in the home of that widow whose cruse of oil the prophet replenished: [1]—a wonderful token

---
[1] 2 Kings iv. 1–7.

of His goodness laid up for the widow—but she was not ready for it. She had not vessels enough to receive God's gift, and so the gift was held back until she should have borrowed from her neighbors. In like manner there are a good many of God's blessings which are *ours*, held by Him for us, but which He cannot give us yet because we are not ready to receive them. They belong to a later point of our experience. It would have been useless to take the Israelites out of Egypt and to set them down at once in the Promised Land. They were not fit to enter at once upon the privileges and duties of citizenship. Just so there are certain gifts of God which mark your life to-day, certain duties, the discharge of which is your highest joy, certain responsibilities under the pressure of which your manhood ripens and grows, which you can very plainly see did not belong to an earlier period. You were not fit to discharge the duties, nor to bear the responsibilities. There are certain views of truth in which you greatly rejoice, which you count it among the best gifts of God to have had revealed to you: and yet you can see, perhaps, that it was far better the revelation should have been delayed. You can understand our Lord's words to the disciples—"I have yet many things to say unto you, but ye cannot bear them now."[1] You can see that the truth was one which it needed some experience to use rightly; that it has sides which you might have magnified unduly and pressed so as to do harm rather than good. In short, it was an instrument which God kept laid up for you, and did not give into your

---

[1] John xvi. 12.

hands until some preparatory discipline and experience had fitted you both to use and to enjoy it.

And it ought not to be forgotten, moreover, that a part of this preparation depends upon ourselves; and that therefore it is sometimes *our* fault that the laid-up goodness is kept back. If we neglect the preparation, we shall fail of the blessing, just as the widow might have thwarted the prophet's intended kindness by refusing to borrow the vessels. A professing Christian, for instance, says—" I wish I enjoyed the public and social church service more than I do. I fairly envy the keen delight with which my neighbor in the next pew enters into song and sermon, and prayer. I have no fault to find with the preaching; I suppose it is good enough, but I don't enjoy my church privileges as I suppose I should." Well, you know David was a man who especially enjoyed the sanctuary. You know how he pined after it when he was in exile; how, even when he was hiding from Saul in the cave, he declared that he would praise the Lord among the people and sing praises among the nations.[1] He will tell you in the fifty-seventh and one hundred and eighth Psalms the secret of his enjoyment. " O God, my heart is fixed [literally *prepared*]. I will sing and give praise, even with my glory."[2] Continually we are hearing this cry from churchgoers—"We are not *interested:*" as if forsooth the preaching of the word and the social means of grace must take them up bodily like so many children, and interest them whether they will or not. Too much of the burden is shifted from the right shoulders. If the pulpit and the prayer-meet-

---

[1] Psalm lvii. 9.   [2] Psalm cviii. 1.

ing are justly chargeable in some instances with the failure to interest, the difficulty is quite as often that men and women come to their ministrations with unprepared hearts, depending upon these to lift them as so much dead weight, and to strike fire out of their iciness. Of course they do not receive the goodness which God has laid up for them in His temple; the interest is all outside of themselves; there is no responsive interest *in* themselves. I have noticed when travelling among the woods and mountains that when a man was really thirsty, he was not very finical about the particular way of getting a drink. If he had a silver drinking-cup with him, he used it of course; but he seemed to drink with no less relish when he had to use a tin-cup, or a cow-horn, or even to lie flat down on the bank and drink from the stream itself. The amount of it was, he was *thirsty;* and people will not drink pure water when they are not thirsty; they want something sweetened or spiced to tickle the palate. Only let our churches be filled with souls *thirsting* for the goodness which God has laid up for them in His word and ordinances, and there will soon be interest enough.

God really consults for our pleasure by His judicious reservation of His bounties. You take a child to a cabinet with six drawers full of pictures and curiosities, and give him the keys of the whole six, and let him rummage them all in one morning, and he will be one of the unhappiest of children. Allow him to open only one each day, or every two days, and you heighten his pleasure. He enjoys more deliberately. He finds more in each drawer than he would in a morning's overhauling of the whole six. Men, like children, are often disposed to want all their happiness at once; and often, when God does send a blessing, they are so annoyed because He did not send something more, that they do not half enjoy what they have. Yet God was wiser than they in keeping something laid up. You would not enjoy travelling over a long road where all the beautiful scenery was crowded into the first mile, leaving twenty miles of barren, flat, dismal country. When you visit Niagara Falls, the whole scene comes to you at once. In a glance you take in the American fall, and Goat Island, and the Horseshoe, and both rapids, and the green, swirling, foam-streaked river below. And yet not a few people prefer the quieter and gradually unfolding beauty of Trenton, where you wind your way up the stream through a succession of fresh and gradually opening views, coming upon fall after fall, at once charmed with the present scene, and lured on by the roar of waters to new beauties beyond. Similarly, God makes a happier, a more beautiful life for us by keeping a part of our blessings laid up in store, by distributing them over a larger surface, by mixing them up with sadder experiences, thus at once tempering the sadness, and keeping prosperity from making us unruly.

Another of God's designs in this policy of reservation, is *to stimulate us to effort.* No one can study the Scriptures long without seeing that God's gifts are to be *sought for*. If our joy is to be full, it is on condition that we *ask.* Christ's disciples were rebuked because they had asked nothing. And there is this peculiarity about God's blessings, that, while they satisfy the *present* need they create *new* needs, and stimulate to fresh search and asking. The Arabian story tells of the young prince who, having squandered his patrimony in dissipation, was directed in a vision to dig up the floor of his chamber; and on doing so discovered a subterranean apartment. On exploring this, he found an urn; and on opening the urn discovered a key. This set him looking for the lock to which the key belonged, and having at last discovered a secret door in the wall, he opened another chamber containing eleven statues of pure gold, and a pedestal for a twelfth, with an inscription bidding him search for the remaining statue. Even so each blessing of God reveals another on beyond, by revealing the *need* of another. When you shall receive a gift which leaves you no wish but to sit down and enjoy it, you may seriously question whether that gift is a blessing from God; since God's blessings always point to the goodness that is *laid up*. We have the truth illustrated in Paul's experience. It was a wonderful display of God's goodness, when he was, as he puts it, "grasped" or "seized" by Christ [1]—snatched from his narrow Jewish prejudices and from his enmity to Christ and to His church. "But," he says, "there was something to be attained after that. I count not myself to have apprehended. When Christ laid hold of me, He lifted me to a height from which I discovered new spiritual treasures to be won, larger knowledge of heavenly things, new enemies to be subdued; and so I forget the things which are behind, and press towards the mark for the prize of my *high* calling; for God is calling me higher and higher, even unto heaven." He was like a man who climbs a peak and looks out over a new conti-

---

[1] Philippians iii. 12.

The Treasury Gate. 99

nent, full of goodness laid up. Take your own experience. Go back to the beginning of your Christian life. How joyful was the sense of forgiven sin. How your whole heart went out in the words of the old Psalm—"Bless the Lord, O my soul, and all that is within me bless His holy name, who forgiveth all thine iniquities."[1] Yet how long was it before that very experience set you seeking for fresh displays of His goodness? It had set you on a track where there was daily work to be done as well as pardoning love to enjoy; and you must needs draw on the goodness laid up for wisdom to map out your work, and for strength to prosecute it. Then, when you had gotten that, you found that your work led you into dark places, and brought you face to face with hard problems, and you were getting weary and discouraged and sorrowful; and there came a large draft on the goodness laid up, for patience, for sympathy, for comfort, for victory; and so it has been all along the course; one experience has led the way to another, and each succeeding one has developed new demands upon the goodness laid up, and new and ever richer revelations of that goodness.

Illustrations of this principle of reserve are seen particularly in God's *promises*, and in His *providences*.

A promise of God seems a very simple thing at first view. So does an acorn. No one who did not know the facts of vegetable life would dream that there is an oak tree enfolded in it. In a single promise are folded an infinite variety of provisions and adaptations, laid up, and not manifesting themselves until they are wanted.

---

[1] Psalm ciii.

It is very much like the tent about which we used to read in the fairy story, which could be shut up in the hand, and yet could be spread out on occasion so as to cover a whole army. When a man takes a promise into his life, he finds it continually developing unsuspected resources. It comes in to help and to comfort him at points where he never dreamed it could be of any service to him. It is something as when an inexperienced traveller goes out for an excursion among the Alps, and is bidden to take a rope with him. He does not exactly see what he is going to want with it, but when he gets upon a snow slope, the guide ties him to himself with the rope; and when he slips into a crevasse, he finds that the rope is all there is between him and death. They come to a steep ledge, and the rope is in demand again. They set up their mountain tent for the night, the rope comes into play. That traveller finds out how many uses are laid up in a rope before he gets back to his lodging. He never will think of going into the mountains again without one. So a Christian takes a familiar promise like "cast thy burden on the Lord, and He shall sustain thee. He shall never suffer the righteous to be moved."[1] When his first little trial or sorrow comes, he falls back on his promise, and he finds that it answers perfectly. By and by troubles thicken, and burdens grow heavier, and he looks round for a promise, and the old one falls under his hand again; and he is surprised to find that it does not bend under the heavier load. And again troubles come in an avalanche. Not only are resources and friends gone, but *he*

---

[1] Psalm lv. 22.

is broken, and he lies a helpless wreck, with hardly strength to grope round for a promise; and when he does, he lights on "he shall sustain thee;" and somehow it never seemed so large and so strong before; and he finds that the same promise which held up his first little care, now bears up the whole mountain of sorrow, and the dead weight of his poor wrecked self into the bargain.

And sometimes Christians go for a good while in trouble through not realizing what riches of goodness are laid up for them in a familiar promise. They are like a foreigner who walks our streets weak and hungry, and who does not know the value of the five dollar bill hidden in his pocket. It is with a shock of surprise that it now and then comes to you as you read that old promise—"why that means me!" When Christian and Hopeful strayed out of the path upon forbidden ground, and found themselves locked up in Despair Castle for their carelessness, there they lay for days, until one night they began to pray. "Now a little before it was day, good Christian, as one half amazed, broke out in this passionate speech: 'What a fool,' quoth he, 'am I, thus to lie in a stinking dungeon, when I may as well walk at liberty. I have a key in my bosom called PROMISE, that will, I am persuaded, open any lock in Doubting Castle.' Then said Hopeful, 'That's good news, good brother; pluck it out of thy bosom and try.' Then Christian pulled it out of his bosom, and began to try at the dungeon door, whose bolt gave back, and the door flew open with ease, and Christian and Hopeful both came out." And what is true of the promises may be applied to the whole word. Away back in David's time men were praising God for the treasures laid up in His word ; and the centuries have passed on, and learning, and genius, and piety have been digging in this mine all the while. There never was so much known about the word of God as there is to-day, and yet never was there such stimulus to farther research : we cannot exhaust it. It is a fountain fed by eternal springs :

> "Its streams the whole creation reach,
> So plenteous is the store :
> Enough for all, enough for each,
> Enough for *evermore!*"

Again, God's goodness is laid up in His providences. Their meaning is not grasped at once, and their result is not reached at once. One of God's dispensations seems like a single act :—a blow, a rending asunder, a blight, a wreck, and it is done ; that is the end of it ; let us get over the consequences as we may. That, I say, is the short-sighted *human* view of the matter ; but that is *not* the end of it. That single dispensation has a wide range. It is in many parts ; and the man who patiently follows God along its line, will see it unfold into new meanings and new bearings upon his life.

> "His purposes will ripen fast,
> Unfolding every hour."

I am not so sure about the *fast* ripening. I am inclined to think that God's purposes often unfold rather slowly, and not hour by hour. But as to the unfolding itself there can be no doubt. Great store of goodness, of love, of beneficent purpose is laid up in these providences which seem so severe, as a gem is sometimes found enclosed in a rough, hard stone. A man who sets himself to watch and to follow the development of one of these providences is like one who watches the unrolling of a rich web from a foreign loom. First appears a rough selvage : then follows a dark, sombre fabric: no beauty there : then, perhaps, a streak of gold or a line of embroidery : then more and more gold and color, until at last the web unfolds its whole pattern, blazing in gold and in gorgeous dyes. So you do not see the gold nor the purple in the first unfolding of God's providence. It is all rough and sad-hued; but the purple and gold are laid up none the less in the heart of the providence : they are of one piece with the sombre web, and God will bring the whole pattern to light by and by to the praise of the great goodness which He has laid up for them that fear Him.

God has strange wrappers for His promises. He lays up His goodness sometimes in strange places. There is one promise of His presence and companionship which lies in the very depth of the waters, and another still which can only be found in the heart of the fire. "When thou passest through the waters I will be with thee. When thou walkest through the fire thou shalt not be burned, neither shall the flame kindle upon thee."[1]

Out of this truth grows a practical admonition which cannot but be serviceable to us as we face the work and trial of the future : an exhortation to faith in God, to patient waiting and hopefulness. There is another clause

---

[1] Isaiah xliii. 2.

to the text—"Which Thou hast wrought before the sons of men for them that trust in Thee." God's goodness is not always kept hidden. If there is *reserve* there is also *unfolding*. If there is laying up of goodness, there is also working it out publicly before men's faces. But if we want the goodness *wrought out*, we must have faith in the goodness which *is laid up*. If we want the performance, we must trust the promise; or, as one has said—"As God's faithfulness engageth us to believe, so our faith, as it were, engageth God's faithfulness to perform the promise."[1] We are often speculating on what is to come; whether the years shall bring life or death, prosperity or sorrow. You ask the watchman, "What of the night?" You who trust Him, you who are His dear children through faith in Jesus Christ, may take this answer as regards the coming years: you are going forth into nothing but *goodness*. "*All things* work together *for good* to them that love God."[2] I cannot say that you may not be going forward into trouble, humiliation, toil, disappointment. It may well be; but I repeat it, if you are walking at God's side, you are going forward to nothing but good: great goodness is laid up for you on the simple condition of your trust in God. Take this truth as a fact and not as a poetic fancy:—God has great goodness laid up for me. If the worst which I fear shall come to pass, I shall find His goodness laid up in the heart of the disaster. If there is some cherished desire yet unfulfilled, for which you have been looking year after year, perhaps it is laid up for a time when the fulfilment will do you more good

---

[1] Nathanael Hurdy, quoted by Spurgeon.　　[2] Romans viii. 28.

than now. Perhaps God's goodness is laid up in *not* fulfilling it: at any rate, follow the line of God's providence whither it leads you, take the good as it falls in along the line, and be thankful as you *know* that, with God as your guide, you cannot be travelling any road which does not lead to something better.

THE GATE TO THE CONFESSIONAL.

PSALM XXXII.

(1) Blessed is he whose transgression is taken away, whose sin is covered :
(2) Blessed is the man to whom Jehovah reckoneth not iniquity,
And in whose spirit there is no guile.
(3) For while I kept silence, my bones waxed old
Through my roaring all the day long.
(4) For day and night Thy hand was heavy upon me ;
My moisture was turned into the drouth of summer.
(5) I would acknowledge my sin unto Thee,
And mine iniquity did I not cover.
I said, I will confess my transgressions unto Jehovah,
And Thou tookest away the iniquity of my sin.
(6) For this cause let every godly man pray to Thee
In a time when Thou mayest be found ;
So surely when the great waters overflow,
They shall not reach him.
(7) Thou art my hiding-place ;
Thou wilt preserve me from trouble ;
Thou wilt compass me about with songs of deliverance.
(8) I will instruct and teach thee in the way thou shouldest go ;
I will watch over thee with mine eye.
(9) Be ye not as horse, or as mule without understanding,
Whose trapping is with bit and bridle to hold them,
Or else they will not come nigh unto thee.
(10) Many sorrows are to the wicked,
But whoso trusteth in Jehovah, loving kindness compasseth him about.
(11) Rejoice in Jehovah and exult, O ye righteous ;
And shout for joy, all ye that are upright in heart.

VII.

THE GATE TO THE CONFESSIONAL.

THE point at which the earlier brilliancy of David's career began to merge in the shadow which overhung his later years, was his fearful sin in the matter of Uriah the Hittite. It was indeed an awful crime or cluster of crimes; yet the shock of his defilement is tempered and relieved for us by the spectacle of his penitence. If we grieve at the weakness which yielded so abjectly to temptation, we cannot but admire the vigor and promptitude with which resolution gathers itself up amid the wreck of character, and with manly sorrow, frank confession, and honest penitence, begins a new life in God's strength. One has truly said, "He is not what he was before; but he is far nobler and greater than many a just man who never fell and never repented. He is far more closely bound up with the sympathies of mankind than if he had never fallen."[1]

It is with this lighter side of the sad history that our Psalm deals. Whatever else it may teach us, it teaches us this broad truth that the forgiven penitent, under *God's* economy, is not a *wretched* man. "*Blessed* is he whose

---

[1] Stanley, Jewish Church.

transgression is forgiven." If the world forgives, it generally vouchsafes a kind of stinging forgiveness which perpetuates the smart of the crime. It is at no pains to *cover* the sin. We can say of one thus forgiven, " He is *tolerated:* he has a new chance given him," but scarcely—" he is blessed." This Psalm, on the contrary, while it is one of the saddest, is at the same time one of the most joyful of the inspired lyrics. It is no less the record of a bitter, penitential sorrow, than the expression of a heart full of praise. It comes to us to-day to tell us that the worst sinner, forgiven by God, is a happy man.

The true *nobility* of repentance shows itself in nothing more impressively than in the willingness it begets to put such sad experience at the disposal of the world for warning and for instruction. It would be but a natural dictate of the heart to cover the sin as God has covered it. It would be the natural prompting of self-interest to say, " The world knows too much already. No need of refreshing its recollection of my short-comings." But, if I may use the words of an old writer—" This is a remark of a true penitent, when he hath been a stumbling-block to others, to be as careful to raise them up by his repentance, as he was hurtful to them by his sin ; and I never think that man truly penitent who is ashamed to teach sinners repentance by his own particular proof. Happy and thrice happy is the man who can build so much as he hath cast down." [1]

In this Psalm, David gives to the world his experience as a sinner. He tells us

---

[1] Archibald Symson, quoted by Spurgeon.

1st.—OF THE BLESSEDNESS OF FORGIVENESS.
2d.—OF THE RESULT OF HIS ATTEMPTS TO COVER HIS SIN.
3d.—OF THE REMEDY WHICH HE FOUND.
4th.—OF THE RESULT OF ITS APPLICATION.
5th.—DRAWS A PRACTICAL LESSON FOR OUR INSTRUCTION.

When a shipwrecked sailor has been rescued from death, and is sitting warm and dry by the fire, his first thought, his first utterance is one of *congratulation*. "How fortunate I am to have escaped. How thankful I am to those who saved my life." After this feeling has found vent, he will go on to tell the story of his shipwreck and of his rescue. Hence nothing could be more natural than the ordering of this Psalm. David is a *rescued* man; and thanksgiving, and congratulation on his present security come to his lips, before he tells the story of his moral shipwreck. He brings the blessedness of the pardoned soul before us under three phases. First, his sin is *taken away*. Perhaps David had in his mind the picture of that strange rite, so often repeated in the wilderness,—the high priest standing with his hands upon the head of the scapegoat, and confessing over it the sins of the people, and the animal led away, with its mystical burden of trangressions, into the wilderness. But whatever the image, that is the *fact* concerning a pardoned soul; its sins are *taken away*. "In those days, and in that time, saith the Lord, the iniquity of Israel shall be sought for, and there shall be none; and the sins of Judah, and they shall not be found."[1]

---

[1] Jeremiah L 20.

Like the entry in a creditor's book, they are blotted out. God does not, indeed, when He takes away sin, agree to take away all the *consequences* of sin. There were certain results of David's sin which even God's forgiveness could not remove. Forgiveness could not set Uriah again in his place in the army or in his household; it could not wipe away the dishonor from his door. There were certain complications in the royal family and in the state—natural outgrowths of David's polygamy, which took their own course, spite of his repentance and his pardon. Amid their sinful indulgences, men should keep it before them that Nature knows nothing of forgiveness. But the utterance of the Psalm concerns sin in its relations to God and to future judgment. As affecting the sinner's relations to these, it is *taken away*. It never will appear against him again: he may fall again, and lower than before; but *those* sins, freely forgiven, will never be laid to his account.

 2d.—He is blessed in that his sins are *covered* or *hidden*, and that from *God;* not from men. There is no real blessedness in the fact that men do not know our sins; and it is worthy of notice that these words strike at the very sentiment underlying the social and moral rottenness which is coming to light so wonderfully in these days: the sentiment that makes men content to live a life which is an awful, hollow cheat in God's sight,—disturbed only by the prospect of detection by their fellow-men, as if the chief end of man were *not to be found out:* as if man's relations to GOD were not first: as if the first thing to be provided for were not the scrutiny of the *divine* eye: as if exposure to the world were not as a grain of sand when weighed against exposure to the eye of Him with whom we *must* deal sooner or late, and to whom "all things are naked and opened."[1] If you would estimate the blessedness of such covering of sin, read the familiar story of Ananias and Sapphira: example for all time of those who would stand well with men at the expense of a lie, without a thought of the God whose service they were caricaturing. *That* thought comes uppermost in the words of the apostle who pronounces their sin and their doom: "Why hath Satan filled thine heart to lie to the Holy Ghost? Thou hast not lied unto men, but unto God."[2] How different the feeling of David. His *sin* is public; the story of his moral fall has spread from the court to the army and through the kingdom: yet there is not a hint of sorrow for that. Nay, as we have seen, he holds up his own sin as a beacon to warn the world. Man's estimate of the matter does not seem to occur to him; but only the joyful fact that it is covered from God: that God *himself* covers it. However men may comment or rail, it matters little while God says "I have blotted out as a thick cloud thy transgressions, and as a cloud thy sins."[3]

3d.—He is blessed still farther in that he *is treated as innocent*. The Lord does not impute nor lay the iniquity to his charge. Paul gives us, in the fourth chapter of Romans, the Christian development of this thought, confirming it by these very words of David. "To him that worketh not, but believeth on Him that justifieth the ungodly, his faith is counted for righteousness." That is, God treats him who, in faith, lays his sins upon Jesus Christ, just as though he were righteous.

---

[1] Hebrews iv. 13. [2] Acts v. 3, 4. [3] Isaiah xliv. 22.

But we notice that there follows a phrase which, if I may so speak, *brackets* all these three. From whom does the Lord take away sin? For whom does He cover it? To whom does He not impute it? Who is this blessed man? He is the one "in whose spirit there is no guile:" not the man who is *innocent*, but he who does not seek to conceal or to extenuate his fault by excuses and subterfuges and self-deceptions. Let us be sure that we put the emphasis in the right place: " Blessed is the man to whom the *Lord* imputeth not iniquity." We are not blessed because we do not impute iniquity to *ourselves;* that is a reckoning with which we cannot be trusted. There is a natural guile in the human heart which always makes it strike the balance on the wrong side ; that is, to its own credit. Men are very much like little children who hide their faces in their hands, fancying that no one sees them, because they do not see themselves. The Spirit gives us a specimen of that kind of self-delusion in the message to the church of Laodicæa. The *church's* reckoning ran thus:—" I am rich and increased with goods, and have need of nothing." The Spirit's reckoning ran thus:—" Thou art wretched and miserable, and poor, and blind, and naked;" and, worst of all, "thou knowest it not."[1] O, remember that sin is not covered because we cover it from ourselves! God covers sin only when man frankly uncovers it. "If we *confess* our sins, He is faithful and just to forgive us our sins, and to cleanse us from all unrighteousness."[2] When man covers, God is sure to discover.

---

[1] Revelation iii. 15-18.   [2] 1 John i. 9.

The Gate to the Confessional. 115

However, men sometimes need experience to teach them this truth, and that was the case with David. He tried the policy of covering his sin, and he gives us the result of the experiment in the following verses. He withheld confession; he kept silence. Perhaps he sought to still that secret voice which was urging him to lay bare his sin, by plunging into the business of state, or into the pleasures of his court; but all in vain. "When I kept silence my bones waxed old." The very seat of strength was invaded. His *body* suffered from the terrors of remorse. What an image is this that follows—the pressure of a strong hand, hampering all free activity. No joy in work or in study any more. The healthy competitions of business, the free play of social converse, the sweet interchanges of the household, all repressed and devitalized by this painful consciousness of guilt. What ails the man who was but late so sparkling, so magnetic, so enthusiastic? "Day and night, THY hand was heavy upon me; my moisture is turned into the drought of summer." The old freshness of heart is gone, like a running stream dried up in the sickening heat of the eastern sun, and leaving nothing but the tasteless details of duty, like the stones and patches of sand in the bed of the brook. Truly has one said, "God's hand is very helpful when it uplifts, but it is awful when it presses down." Has David read your heart? Has David told your story? Have you had any better success in keeping silence, and in trying to cover your sin, than he had? If not, you must be looking for relief by this time. If not, *anything* must be thrice welcome which will take off the pressure of that heavy hand, and set the springs of your freshness running again in your heart. You can do no better now than to keep by David, and to seek relief where he sought it. *What, then, was his remedy?*

It was *confession*. "I acknowledged my sin unto Thee, and mine iniquity have I not hid. I said, I will confess my transgressions unto the Lord." This, David tells us, is a very effective medicine. Let us analyze its properties a little. We find it, all through Scripture, prescribed as the necessary preliminary to forgiveness. "Speak unto the children of Israel," says God to Moses, "when a man or woman shall commit any sin that men commit to do a trespass against the Lord, and that person be guilty, then they shall *confess* their sin which they have done."[1] "He that covereth his sins," says Solomon, "shall not prosper; but whoso *confesseth* them, and forsaketh them, shall have mercy."[2]

"Well," you say, "if God knows all about my sin, why should I confess it?" God knows what you want in prayer before you ask Him, and yet you will not get it if you do not ask Him. He has conditioned forgiveness upon confession, just as He has conditioned finding upon seeking.

But besides this, you are to remember that the mere mention of the fact of your sin before God does not constitute confession. It is, indeed, nothing for you to repeat to Him a fact which He knows perfectly well; but true confession implies your *viewing that fact in the same light in which God views it.* Your little boy gets angry and strikes his brother. You call him to you and say,

---

[1] Numbers v. 6, 7. [2] Proverbs xxviii. 13.

"Did you strike your brother?" "Yes, I struck him." "My son, you have done wrong. You have shown a wicked spirit. Your brother provoked you, but you should have returned good for evil. Is not that so? Don't you see that you did wrong?" And the boy shuts his teeth hard, and says, "No, it was right. He hurt me, and I punished him. When I get a chance I will strike him again." Now, the boy has confessed the act, but you see very clearly that you cannot forgive him so long as he insists that the act was right. You will most assuredly punish him if he do not come to you and say, "Father, I *did* wrong. My temper was very wicked. I *deserve* to be punished." And just so you may go to God and rehearse the whole catalogue of your misdeeds in detail; but you may just as well spare your breath if you are not ready to acknowledge the *guilt* of your acts, as well as the acts themselves. God will have the declaration from your own lips, that you are a transgressor at every point where He charges you with transgression; that every defence is broken down; that your most cherished and most stoutly defended sin is just what His Word declares it to be—ugly and without excuse; that the law has a just charge against you, and that God is fully justified in every word of condemnation which he utters against you. That is the way in which David viewed it, as appears from his words in the fifty-first Psalm, which grew out of this same sin. "Against THEE, THEE, ONLY, have I sinned, and done this evil in THY sight, *that Thou mightest be justified when Thou speakest, and be clear when Thou judgest.*"

Again, let it be remembered that confession implies *re-*

nunciation. When a hardened criminal in his cell gleefully recounts to his visitor or lawyer the details of his wicked life, that is not a confession which commends him to mercy. The man who makes formal acknowledgment of his sins to God, knowing in his secret heart that he is going forth to do the same deeds again, is only mocking and defying God.

And, once more: True confession is not something *extorted* by terror and by fear of impending justice. Such an acknowledgment implies only fear and despair. It is not the utterance of a man who arises and goes to his father, but of one whom bailiffs arrest while he flees from his father. True confession implies faith in God's pardoning grace, and confidence in his power to make the broken bones rejoice, and to wash the tainted heart whiter than snow. It is a voluntary laying bare of the wound to the eye of a trusted surgeon.

Confession, therefore, as implying godly sorrow and true repentance, is David's remedy in this strait. The Prodigals of the Old and of the New Testament answer to each other: "I will confess my transgressions unto the Lord." "I will arise and go to my father, and will say unto him, Father, I have sinned against heaven and before thee."[1]

And now, how does the remedy work in David's case?

He first sums up the result in a single sentence: "Thou forgavest the iniquity of my sin." He has a whole catalogue of joyful consequences of his confession to present to us; but he is careful to make it perfectly clear at the outset

---

[1] Luke xv. 18.

that all these consequences are linked with forgiveness. The man is not blessed who can *forget* his sins; who can *blind himself* to them; who can *divert his mind* from them; who can temporarily *escape their consequences*. Blessed is he, and *only* he, whose transgression is *forgiven*. Thus we get back to the key-note of the Psalm.

And now what a sudden change reveals itself. The tone of the last few verses has been like the sigh of the wind through the dry valleys. Now we begin to hear the running of streams. The abject penitent, moaning day and night under God's heavy hand, is transformed into a joyful singer of praises; a prophet, with a fresh lesson of God's goodness kindling on his lips. As in every case of true spiritual restoration, the subject's thought goes beyond himself. This experience of mine shall be the experience of every one who fears God. "For this shall every one that is godly pray unto thee in a time when thou mayest be found." For *this;* because such has been my blessed experience. And yet there is an undercurrent of warning mingling with the note of praise: "in a time when Thou mayest be found." There are then times of finding God; and, by implication, times when He may not be found. You ask, is this indeed so? May not God be found at *any* time? I reply, God is *always* the same. His promise *never* varies: "If thou shalt seek the Lord thy God, thou shalt find Him, if thou seek Him with all thy heart and with all thy soul."[1] But you have not unfrequently known cases where, though something you much desired to find was in its right place,

---

[1] Deuteronomy iv. 29.

yet through some forgetfulness or confusion or carelessness on your part you could not find it. So, one may incapacitate himself for fulfilling the condition upon which God promises to be found. He may resist His Spirit until he shall have no disposition to seek Him; no disposition to repent and to confess. " God," says Coleridge, "'has promised pardon on penitence; but has He promised *penitence on sin*? Is the repentance, the passing into a new and contrary principle of action, in the sinner's own power? at his own liking? Has he but to open his eyes to the sin, and the tears are close at hand to wash it away? Verily the tenet of transubstantiation is scarcely at greater variance with the common-sense and experience of mankind, than this self-change as the easy means of self salvation."[1] It is not safe to struggle away from the pressure of God's hand. Not safe to let those times slip by when God seems so near, when conscience is so sensitive, and perception of Divine truth and of one's own condition as a sinner so clear. It is better to uncover the sin at once. When the sin is uncovered, God is discovered. The hiding of the sin hides God.

But, apart from this warning, the tone of the Psalmist is joyful to the very end. I have escaped from the pressure of the hand that was heavy upon me. Whereas it bore me down, now I lean upon it, and it leads me into pastures of peace, and folds me like a tired child to my Father's heart. I no longer fear the impending judgment of God. In he floods of great waters, in the time when

---

[1] Aids to Reflection.

Divine wrath shall swallow up the rebellious sons of men as in a whirlpool, the floods shall not come nigh me. While the ungodly shall be calling upon rocks and mountains to fall on them and hide them from His face, I will go to Him, my Rock and my Fortress, and hide myself in Him. "Thou art my hiding-place." Thou from whom I strove of late to hide, shalt now hide me Thyself in the secret of Thy tabernacle. Thy word was of late my dread. Sharper than any two-edged sword, it divided soul and spirit, and pierced me with a thousand pangs: but now "I hope in Thy word." I feared but just now that Thou wouldst destroy me. Thy lightnings were terrible: the sound of Thy thundering made me sick at heart: I shrank from Thy step as from the tread of an avenger and destroyer: Thou wert my trouble when I remembered Thee. But THOU—the same God, "*Thou* shalt *preserve me* from trouble." Thou from whose voice I fled like Adam in the garden, "Thou shalt fence me about with *songs:*" whithersoever I turn I shall see Thy hand and hear Thy voice, and shall see and hear only to break forth into an answering song of praise and thanksgiving. See what God can do for a sinner. Look at this sinful, defiled soul, but now wallowing in his lust, raging and smiting in his passion, blighting the fairest flowers of domestic peace in his selfishness, crushed and withered by remorse, groaning under God's hand—and say if anything but Divine grace, Divine compassion, Divine forgiveness can change such an one into the joyful singer of praises who speaks to us to-day through this familiar Psalm.

And the legitimate result of every such experience is to

make its subject a teacher. Christ bade Peter make use of his own terrible sifting to strengthen his brethren.[1] David anticipates the lesson; and these words of his have been the text-book of penitent souls from his time to the present. "I will instruct thee and teach thee in the way which thou shalt go;" this way of repentance and confession in which I have walked. Be not obstinate in refusing to walk therein. Heed my experience, ye who feel the pressure of God's hand, whose moisture is turned into the drought of summer. "Be not like the horses and the mules without understanding, whose ornaments are bridle and bit for restraint, because they do not come near unto thee." That is a terrible comparison. Think of it for a moment. The bridle which *restrains* the beast is its *ornament.* It is a well-known fact that certain animals have a delight in gaudy trappings,[2] and yet these very things are the signs of their *degradation;* proofs that they cannot be appealed to on the grounds of reason and of conscience. And it is also true that the rebellious attitude which a sinful man assumes towards God, is often his *pride.* He tells his companions he is too wise to yield to such foolish notions: too strong to be frightened by those "painted devils"—death and judgment; too far-seeing to have his reason cramped and fettered by such nonsense as repentance and faith: too free to be in subjection to any power in heaven or on earth.

---

[1] Luke xxii. 32.
[2] *Ruodi.* "How well the collar graces that cow's neck!"
Kuoni. "She knows, as well as you, that she's the leader,
And, should I strip it off, she'd cease to eat."
Schiller's "Wilhelm Tell," Act i. Scene 1.

The Gate to the Confessional.

And yet, if he but knew it, this very attitude is his humiliation. It stamps him as an unreasoning creature which does not appreciate its relations to God and to eternity. God would gladly deal with him on noble and generous terms, as a free man in Christ Jesus: would fain guide him by His eye : says to him, " Come, and let us *reason together :*" but if man refuses, he must be dealt with on other terms. If he will not accept the guidance of the eye, he must take up with that of the bit and bridle. God appealed to Pharaoh first as a man, with fair reasoning and respectful solicitation ; and this failing, he was treated as a lower creature, and animals and insects became the instruments of his torment. If men will not come nigh unto God and fall in with His economy, they must be restrained from interfering with it.

The two conditions are before us. They are summed up for us by the Psalmist himself as the result of his own painful experience of sin, and of his joyful experience of forgiveness and salvation. Many sorrows shall be to the wicked; but he that trusteth in the Lord, mercy shall compass him about." The two pictures are before us, we can judge for ourselves. Shall we have the dryness and the mourning, the blackness of guilt, the pressure of the heavy hand, the terror and dread of God, the restraint of bit and bridle,—or the confession and submission, the songs of deliverance, the joy of forgiveness, the guidance of the eye, the hiding-place in God, the shout of the upright in heart?

THE GATE TO THE WAITING-PLACE.

PSALM XXXVII.

(7) Rest in the Lord and wait patiently for Him : fret not thyself because of Him who prospereth in his way, because of the man who bringeth wicked devices to pass.

VIII.

THE GATE TO THE WAITING-PLACE.

MEN who live selfish lives, walking according to the course of this world, are very apt to take a comfortable view of the condition of society, at least so long as they themselves are happy and prosperous. "It is a very good kind of world after all," they will tell you: "there is a great deal in it that is enjoyable, and a great deal of its evil is exaggerated." Such sentiments are very often the expression of a selfishness which *cares* very little about the condition and tendencies of society, or of a blindness and ignorance which *know* very little about its condition and tendencies.

When a man has once come into right relations with God, has begun to live for others rather than for self, has begun to seek "the kingdom of God and His righteousness," and that not for himself only, but for his fellow-men, when his desires are summed up in the prayer—"Thy kingdom come," he is apt to grow uneasy as he sees how slow the Divine kingdom is in coming, and how many indications there are of the presence and tremendous power of another and hostile kingdom in society.

This Psalm is addressed to a soul which is confused and alarmed by this aspect of the world. It clearly recognizes the facts which make it uneasy and tempt it to fretfulness. Hints of them are scattered from one end of it to the other. The very first verse recognizes the presence and work of evil-doers. They plot against the just; they watch the righteous : they lie in wait to slay him. Not only so, they *succeed*. They bring wicked devices *to pass*. They are in *great* power, and spread themselves like green bay trees. Good men are slandered, pure reputations are blackened, the helpless and the innocent fall under the harrow of the wicked and the designing. From such facts the thought runs naturally to the whole great mystery of God's administration in the world. *God's* administration ! So dire is the confusion at times, so sharp the contradiction, so baffling the mystery of providence, so imperceptible the progress of truth and of virtue, that the hold of the strongest faith trembles, and the spectral doubt thrusts its leering lineaments into the face of God's child— "*Do* all things indeed work together for good ?" It is not only that wickedness is rampant, but that goodness is tainted; that good men are weak, and bigoted, and most positive and aggressive where they should be most humble and docile ; that the very men and women who seem most necessary are stricken down ; that

> "The good die first,
> While those whose hearts are dry as summer dust
> Burn to the socket ;"

that in *religion*, no less than in worldly things, men are carried away by the shallow, the plausible, and the transient, rather than anchored to the deep, abiding, eternal truth.

While the Psalm opens to us this picture—and it is as

The Gate to the Waiting-Place. 129

old as human society, and has tortured the minds of good and true men from the beginning of time,—it also puts us in the right attitude towards this mystery and confusion. Over against it all it sets the great truth—" GOD REIGNS," and the consequent precept—" TRUST IN HIM." To the man who is thus troubled, and anxious, and tempted to fret, it says—" Fret not thyself. Society, lawless, aimless as it appears, is held in God's hand. Leave it there: labor to improve your corner of it: do good in your own day and generation: instead of despairing, *trust* in the Lord: instead of fretting, *delight* yourself in God: instead of being restless, *rest* in the Lord: hold thou still in Jehovah: He shall bring it to pass."

"Yes," is the reply, "but He is *so long* in bringing it to pass: He makes me wait so long." So He does, and probably will; and it is this side of the lesson of faith in God which I want to bring out of this Psalm—the lesson of *waiting*.

For that is the side of faith which develops most slowly. *Working* is not always a sign of faith. There are certain natures to which work is an instinct and a necessity ; and such usually turn to work in times of sorrow or trouble, to "*work it off*," as they say. But if a man merely *diverts* his mind from trouble, or *forgets* trouble in work, his relief is *work*, not *God*." Diversion and oblivion are not faith. Successful work involves no faith ; it is only joy. Faith's harder lesson is given in making a man lie still, and not work at all, but simply bear and wait ; it is given in God's both smiting him and tying his hands ; in his being forced to stand still and see wrong consummated, and villainy successful, and the wicked in great power;

6*

it is given in his being compelled to work without success, as men style it; to labor for consummations which God indefinitely postpones; it is under such discipline that he wants GOD, no one less, to say to him, "Hold thou still in Jehovah, and wait patiently for Him."

As we go through the Psalm, we may gather out of it several thoughts which illustrate and enforce this idea of waiting.

We are to wait *unwaveringly*. In the thirty-fourth verse we read, "Wait on the Lord *and keep His way.*" God brings men to His consummations *only by His own road*. Whatever *apparent* prosperity they may reach by other roads, no matter how long, is not of God's giving; and therefore, no matter how tedious God's way is, or how tortuous, or how long God keeps them walking in it, they are to keep *His* way if they would win His good. And this is often a severe trial of faith. It is as when one has been travelling for long hours over a rough road, amid storm and mist, with night drawing on, looking, as he gains the top of every successive hill, for the spires of the city to which he is going, and seeing instead only a new stretch of dreary road, and a new hill to be climbed—he is tempted to think his guide has lost the way, and to take matters into his own hands. To the man who waits on God it is indispensable that he trust his guide. Having committed his way unto the Lord as he is bidden in the fifth verse, he is to bear always in mind the assurance of the twenty-third verse that "the steps of a good man are *ordered* of the Lord." The Lord will not order one step too many; He will not order one step in the wrong direction; but men on God's road are often tempted, as they are on country roads,

The Gate to the Waiting-Place. 131

by the alluring promise of short-cuts. They think they see a short way to success—to wealth, reputation, social reform—and into it they rush, and go on smoothly enough for awhile only to find themselves at last in some treacherous bog, where reputation and wealth are swamped, and reform is retarded, and the true good is farther off than ever.

Again, while men are often *tempted* into wavering from God's way, they are also often *scared* into wavering. God's way is a safe way to the man who keeps in it. "He that walketh uprightly walketh *surely;*"[1] but God's way nevertheless leads *through* dangers. Daniel found it so when it led him to the mouth of the lions' den, and *into* it. The three Hebrews found it so, when it led into Nebuchadnezzar's furnace. Paul found it so when it lay through the flying stones of the Lystran mob; and no Christian ever tries to walk God's road without the risk of being scared from duty. It may not be by the threat of coarse and brutal persecution, but it will be by influences just as potent. It costs money sometimes for a man to be true to God; it costs the displeasure of good men sometimes for a man to hold to God's methods, and to refuse to adopt shorter and more plausible ones which promise a quicker result. Not a few men are entrapped into indorsing what their deepest convictions condemn, by the fear of seeming to oppose a good work. There is more real courage and close cleaving to God's way than is often supposed, among *heretics* so called.

---

[1] Proverbs x. 9.

"There lives more faith in honest doubt,
Believe me, than in half the creeds."

To human reason, safety lies in stepping out of God's way when these dangers appear ; to faith safety lies only in *keeping* in His way. By stepping out he may save his reputation, his money, his social standing, his reputation for *orthodoxy;* but by keeping in he will save his *manhood,* his *life,* his *soul.*

To wait on the Lord rightly is to wait *cheerfully.*

"Fret not thyself," says the Psalmist in the first verse, "because of evil-doers ; " and again in the eighth verse, "cease from anger and forsake wrath, fret not thyself in any wise to do evil." You have seen two children bidden by their parent to wait in a certain place for an hour, until he should return, or until some promised pleasure should be prepared : and you have seen the one cheerfully occupy himself with a book or with some object at hand, while the other, though he obeyed the command to remain, fretted, and watched the clock, and wondered when father would return, and was angry because he did not come sooner, and began to fear that he would not come at all, and so made himself generally miserable until the hour had expired. Thus, obedience is not always *cheerful;* and just in proportion to its lack of this element, it is defective. For obedience is of the very nature of faith. In the New Testament, to obey and to believe are the same word ; and true faith is always cheerful and restful, busying itself with the *present* good while it waits for the *promised* good, trusting in the Lord and doing good, and never doubting that the promised good will come in God's own time. Whereas some of God's children, when He asks them to wait for Him, are like a boy at boarding-school when his letter from home fails to come at the usual time. The first day he is uneasy; the second day he spends all his spare time running to the post-office; the third day he is very tearful and woe-begone, and is beginning to think his parents are very cruel and negligent to forget him in that way. The fourth day the letter comes, full of love and of pleasant tidings, and the little fellow is heartily ashamed at having distrusted his parents' affection. You must have noticed the difference in Elijah's behavior at two different crises of his life. On Carmel, after God had sent down fire upon the sacrifice, the prophet went up to pray for rain. God had answered by fire, and he believed He would answer by water. Faith heard the sound of "the tread of the rain," and yet God made Elijah wait. He prayed, and sent his servant to look toward the sea, and there was not a cloud. He prayed again and sent the servant, and still the skies were as brass; and again, and still again, to the seventh time, when the cloud was seen no bigger than a hand; and meanwhile not a word of impatience, murmuring or distrust. But a little later came Jezebel's threat, and Elijah fled into the wilderness, and sat down under a juniper tree and prayed to die. God was too slow for him then. He did not vindicate His power at once; He did not lay His hand on that vile queen, but let her rage and send out her messengers of wrath, and slay the prophets; and Israel, too, showed no sign of spiritual life. They had forsaken God's covenant and thrown down His altars. The revival was too long in coming, and he cried "It is enough; now, O Lord, take away my life." That is the spirit which, now and then, gets the better of not a few of God's children — a spirit half despairing, half angry, which says, "If God cannot show me any better result of my life and work than this, He may as well take me out of the world and have done with it;" and after we have fretted and chafed awhile, and have wasted precious days moping in secret places, like Elijah in his cave, we are very likely to get God's message to Elijah—that still, small voice of authority, not bidding us die, but saying, "What dost thou *here?* go, return on thy way." O how often we need reminding that "he that believeth shall not make haste."[1] Some one tells a story of visiting an insane asylum, where there was a patient, but slightly deranged, who occupied himself with taking apart and putting together watches. One day, without a moment's warning, he was seized with a fit of frenzy, and, snatching the watches, dashed one after the other upon the floor. When he was removed to another room and had become more quiet, the physician said, "How came you to destroy your favorite watches, so much as you loved them and so quiet as you are?" The poor patient replied, in a tone of piercing agony—"I could not bear the tick, tick, ticking, and so I dashed them on the pavement."[2] And so it is with us if we employ our waiting time in brooding and counting the minutes of God's delay, looking painfully out at the windows, and straining the ear to catch the sound of His chariot-wheels, keeping our thought fastened on the *delay*, and not on God, and on the work which God sends to occupy the time of His delay.

---

[1] Isaiah xxviii. 16.   [2] From Spurgeon's "Treasury of David."

The "tick, tick," will drive us into rebellious and angry thoughts and presumptuous words. But if we can only get firm hold of that truth in the thirty-first Psalm—"My times are in Thy hand," if we can leave off looking at the *watch*, and fix our eyes on the Hand that holds it, if we shall stop brooding over delay, and rest in the thought that we and the delay are alike in God's hand, if we shall assure ourselves that, however long this or that development of God's providence may be in coming round, *God himself* is ours here, and now, and forever—that will be rest indeed. "*My* times are in Thy hand." Why, we have no trouble at all about the natural succession of times. Spring, it is true, is a little late now and then, or frost comes a little earlier than usual, but we never think that the course of nature is going to be overthrown. We have no doubt that the crocuses will be found in the woods, and the time of the singing of birds come, and the green forests in due season glow with autumn purple and gold: and why should we be any more troubled about delays in providence? It is all one economy. The distinction between nature and providence is artificial. You and I move in an order as fixed as the order of the seasons, and controlled by the same hand; *our* times as well as *nature's* times are in His hand; may we not wait as cheerfully and hopefully for the late coming providence as for the late spring?

And we have no more business to fret at the times we live in than we have at the delays of Providence. A good many people who *dare* not grumble at Providence, make it up by grumbling at the times. Try as hard as we may to make the age better, we shall not revolutionize it at once, and why not accept the fact, do the best and most we can with a cheerful spirit, and then, with equal cheerfulness, wait for God to make right what we cannot help? But this cheerful waiting seems to be unknown in the experience of some Christians. They wait, they pray, they work, but they fret and scold enough to well nigh spoil both work and prayer. They harp on the degeneracy of the times; they muse on the days of old, and tell us the former days were better than these; they predict ruin and disaster to Church and State; they are in a continuous state of fury against the enemies of religion and of social order. Does it do any good? The Psalmist says not: "Fret not thyself in any wise *to do evil;*" that is, evil will be the result of thy fretting. And it will. An angry state of the heart is a bad thing for the spiritual life; it throws it off its balance; it impairs its power of seeing and estimating truly; it indisposes the soul to communion with God; it tends to make men unjust and uncharitable and despondent and listless. A man cannot carry round with him such a raging fire in his bosom, and at the same time trust in the Lord and do good, and delight himself in the Lord. From being angry at men and things, the transition is easy to suspecting the wisdom of God. No, there is much to sadden us no doubt; much which is adapted to excite indignation, much which is tediously long in righting itself. We are not the only men who have felt the pressure and sadness of the long delay. We are waiting still for what David waited for; but then we are waiting with our faces toward sunrise. The night is farther on now than then; the windows in God's prophecy all open on the east, and over against all the causes of despondency and wrath we have this: "*He shall bring it to pass*," and on the strength of that promise, God bids us look out on the night like one who opens a window which commands a sleeping city, reeking with its wickedness and filth and disease, and who for the moment lifts his eyes above its dark, pestilential streets, and sees the encircling mountains reddening in the fast coming dawn.

And therefore, we may wait *confidently*. The Psalm backs its exhortations by numerous promises. "Thou shalt dwell in the land and verily thou shalt be fed." "He shall give thee the desires of thine heart." "He shall bring forth thy righteousness as the light, and thy judgment as the noonday." "The righteous shall inherit the land and dwell therein forever." Look especially at the twenty-third verse. We have been watching the course of a man in God's way—a traveller who is long in coming to the end—on whom God's providence imposes various and trying delays. To the eye of reason it seems as though the man were walking aimlessly; as though his life, with its continual interruption, and confusion, and stumbling, and baffling, were an utter, irredeemable failure. And so it seems not only to reason, but to weak faith. There have come times to most of us when we have lost out of our lives all sense of plan or order, and have just gone on from day to day, doing and taking what the day brought with it. We have thought, I say, that those were *disordered* periods. They were not. Did you ever study the waves of the ocean? If so, you have noticed that each wave was full of little, irregular swirlings and eddies, moving in all possible directions. And if you could fasten your eyes upon a square foot of that water and shut out all the rest, you might say that it was a mere watery chaos; but when your eye takes in the whole wave, you see that a common movement propels its whole mass, and takes up into itself all these minor movements, and bears them on with the regularity of a marching host. So these spaces of apparent confusion in our lives are not *out of order.* They are carried on in the larger order of God's plan. Perhaps we cannot, *usually* we cannot see the whole movement, but it bears steadily and continuously onward, every incident, every crossing and confusion of incidents swept on at God's own rate and in nice adjustment with God's own plan. There is *no* disorder in the life of the man who walks steadfastly in God's way. "The steps of a good man are *ordered* by the Lord, and he *delighteth* in his way. Though he fall he shall not be utterly cast down, for the Lord upholdeth him with *His* hand." Aye, he *delighteth* in his way; even in that way which is so full of stumbles and falls; that way where we spend so much time in repairing damages. If you are disposed to doubt it, just put yourself back to the days when that stalwart, manly son of yours began to walk. You remember well the first day he staggered to his feet and timidly put one foot before the other. You remember how you delighted in that tottering, uncertain way, with its frequent stumbles. You remember how you saw in those timid steps the promise of the strong, manly stride of the vigorous youth and man; and you remember, too, how you upheld the tottering child with *your* hand and raised him tenderly up when he fell, not to *save* him from walking, but to set him up to walk again. Does your Father in Heaven any less delight in *your* way because it is a feeble, uncertain going? Does He any more leave you to yourself when you fall? Does He any less see and rejoice in the promise of that day when you shall walk with a steady step among the strong sons of God, on the King's highway of holiness?

Mark too that the *steps* are ordered. The *whole* way is ordered it is true, but ordered through the steps. Human philosophy says that the world is moved in the mass, and that the mass carries the details helplessly along with it. *Divine* philosophy says the mass is moved by the details. Just as gravitation acts upon each separate particle of the stone which rolls down the mountainside, so God's *general* providence reaches its result through the *special* providences.[1] The philosopher sneers at the marking of the sparrow's fall; but it is in the ordering of just such details that God fulfils Himself in history. So our lives are what their details are. The goal is reached by God's ordering of their separate steps. The only thing we are to be careful about is that we step each time in God's track. We see only a little of the way in front; we have got to make our way by single steps, if we make it at all; and though God checks our steps, and turns our steps in strange directions, makes us step now and then off what seems to us solid ground, upon what seems like treacherous soil, makes us wait, and wait, and wait in our slow stepping for the appearance of the promised goal—all is well if we only hold fast the truth that each step is in the line of a Divine order, and that the

---

[1] Dr. Mark Hopkins, "Evidences of Christianity," Lect. III.

way by which God leads us, though it seem like threading a hopeless labyrinth, is the way in which He delights, because it leads up to Him.

Rest in the Lord then. Hold thou still in Jehovah and wait patiently for Him. Whether He bid thee stand still, or wait in working for the long delayed end—wait thou *unwaveringly*, keeping His way, and not turning aside to thine own; wait thou *cheerfully*, not fretting thyself in any wise to do evil; wait thou *confidently*, trusting in Him to bring His perfect will to pass, and to cast down every vain thing which exalteth itself against God. Are you unable to make plans? Does the outlook seem dark and confused? Move on step by step then, for your *steps* are ordered by Him. Are you waiting for time to vindicate your reputation, and to disperse the mists in which malice and slander have shrouded your name? Trust in Him, "and He shall bring forth thy righteousness as the light, and thy judgment as the noonday."

> "To God thy way commending,
>   Trust Him whose arm of might,
> The heavenly circles bending,
>   Guides every star aright;
> The winds, and clouds, and lightning,
>   By His sure hand are led;
> And He will, dark shades brightening,
>   Show thee what path to tread.
>
> Trust, with a faith untiring,
>   In thine omniscient King;
> And thou shalt see, admiring,
>   What He to light will bring.

The Gate to the Waiting-Place.

Of all thy griefs the reason
    Shall at the last appear;
Why now denied a season,
    Will shine in letters clear.

Then raise thine eyes to heaven,
    Thou who canst *trust His frown;*
Thence shall thy meed be given,
    The chaplet and the crown:
Thy God the palm victorious
    In thy right hand shall plant,
Whilst thou, in accents glorious,
    Melodious hymns shall chant.—PAUL GERHARD.

THE GATE TO THE PHYSICIAN'S.

PSALM XLII.

(1) As a hart which panteth after the water brooks,
   So panteth my soul after thee, O God.
(2) My soul is athirst for God, for the living God :
   When shall I come and appear before God ?
(3) My tears have been my food day and night,
   While they say unto me continually, Where is thy God ?
(4) These things would I remember, and pour out my soul in me,—
   How I passed with the (festal) throng,
   How I led them in procession to the house of God,
   With the voice of loud song and thanksgiving—a multitude keeping holy day.
(5) Why art thou bowed down, O my soul,
   And (why) art thou disquieted in me ?
   Hope in God ; for I shall yet give Him thanks,
   Who is the health of my countenance and my God.
(6) My God, my soul is bowed down in me ;
   Therefore do I remember Thee from the land of Jordan,
   And from the Hermons, from the mountain of Mizar.
(7) Deep calleth unto deep at the voice of Thy cataracts ;
   All Thy breakers and Thy billows have passed over me.
(8) Yet in the daytime will Jehovah command His lovingkindness;
   And in the night His song (will be) with me,
   A prayer unto the God of my life.
(9) (So) will I say unto God my Rock, " Why hast Thou forgotten me ?
   Why go I mourning because of the oppression of the enemy ? "
(10) As though they would break my bones mine enemies reproach me,
   While they say unto me all day long, " Where is thy God ?"
(11) Why art thou bowed down, O my soul,
   And (why) art thou disquieted in me ?
   Hope in God ; for I shall yet praise Him,
   (Who is) the health of my countenance, and my God.

IX.

THE GATE TO THE PHYSICIAN'S.

PERHAPS somebody will one day write a book which shall gather up the services which unknown men have rendered to their race. Among these the author will surely include this forty-second Psalm. It has been, for centuries, one of the most powerful cordials for the heart-sick and despondent, and its virtue has grown rather than diminished with the lapse of years, and yet we do not know its author, nor its date, nor the peculiar circumstances under which it was written. All we know is that it is the utterance of some one in deep trouble, and that it tells us how he found comfort, and how we may find it under similar circumstances.

The Psalm presents to us first, a picture of extreme despondency, through a succession of graphic figures. First, we have the beautiful gazelle of the desert standing, with panting sides, by the dry watercourses which cleave the mountain range on the east of the Jordan. Dr. Thompson says that he has seen large flocks of these shy creatures gathered by the valley streams in the great deserts of central Syria, so subdued by thirst that they could be approached quite nearly before they fled.

The writer of the Psalm was, apparently, an exile in this mountain region, in sight of the familiar scenes of worship and of domestic tranquillity, and his soul is in great trouble because he is cut off from the sanctuary and from the privileges of public worship. His longing for these is an *intense thirst*, like that of the hart for the water brooks. It is easy for us to say that God's presence is not dependent upon the sanctuary, and that the Psalmist need not have wanted the light of God's countenance even in his exile; but we are to remember that, under the old economy, men depended more upon the form and medium of worship than we do; and that, therefore, the absence of these helps was more keenly felt. And even *we* are not so independent of these forms that we do not seriously feel their absence. Pure spiritual worship is a very easy thing to a pure spirit, but we who are in the flesh do not very often get above the need of sensible helps. Our humanity craves the aid of a few visible, tangible steps under us in our efforts to mount heavenward. Some of us have not been altogether out of sympathy with the Psalmist's thirst, when circumstances have separated us from the familiar scenes of worship. As the weeks rolled on, we have found our heart gathering up its deep feeling in the words of the eighty-fourth Psalm: "How amiable are Thy tabernacles, O Lord of hosts! My soul longeth, yea even fainteth for the courts of the Lord. My heart and my flesh crieth out for the living God." Moreover, we must not forget another important element of the Psalmist's distress. In his day men were accustomed to look for *sensible* tokens of the Divine favor or displeasure. If a man was prosperous, he regarded himself as blessed of God; if he was afflicted, his first feeling was that he had incurred God's displeasure. Hence the writer may, very naturally, have associated his exile with God's anger, and have regarded his banishment from the sanctuary as a banishment from God's favor; at any rate this feeling would be strong enough to awaken a tormenting doubt in his mind, and the consequent thirst for God of which he here speaks.

However the psalmist may have regarded it, his enemies were only too glad to put this construction upon it. Yes, God had forsaken him; the man who was wont to make his boast in the Lord; the man on whom God had showered visible tokens of his favor—God had proved false to him at last. God had left him to wander alone in the wilderness; and so their reproach was murder in his bones, because it allied itself to the doubt in his own soul. They gave utterance, with their taunts, to the very thought against which his weak faith was, perhaps, struggling:—Where is thy God? Why does He not come and help thee? It was the very same sarcasm which the priests and scribes hurled at the crucified Lord: "He trusted in God; let Him deliver him now, if He will have him; for he said, 'I am the Son of God.'"[1]

Added to this is the remembrance of past joys, all the sweeter now that they are gone. Indeed,

> "This *is* truth the poet sings,
> That a sorrow's crown of sorrow, is remembering happier things."

Those old days in the sanctuary—how sweet they were! When I went with the multitude to the house of God, with the voice of joy and praise, with a multitude that

---
[1] Matthew xxvii. 43.

kept holy-day. Shall those days ever come again? My soul thirsteth for God—for the living God. When shall I come and appear before God?

Another picture. Stand by the sea-coast of Palestine on some windy day, and watch the clouds which hang like a pall along the horizon. Now, suddenly, you shall see on the skirts of the clouds, a mass of black vapor, shaped like a long funnel, its smaller end resting on the sea, and the whole mass at once whirling on its own axis, and driven on by the wind with a terrific roar. Look down now at the sea, and behold how the commotion of its surface answers to the commotion above. Where the water-spout moves with its roar, the deep lifts up its voice in an answering roar. " Deep calleth unto deep at the noise of Thy water-spouts." And when these spouts break, as they do sometimes, on the mountains, then woe to the harvests and to the flocks. The dry beds of the streams are swollen in a few minutes into furious rivers— cataracts, whose waves and billows go over grain and olives, sheep and goats, and men, and sweep them away to destruction. The tumult and distress in the Psalmist's soul could only be described by such a picture as this— flood calling unto flood; wave after wave sweeping away his harvest of hope; doubts and fears within answering to calamity without, as the deep to the water-spout. In the exaggeration of sorrow and terror, he puts it as though all God's chastisements had been massed upon him:—" *All Thy waves and Thy billows have gone over me.*"

Thus much for the disease. The picture is sad enough to move our compassion, and true enough to our own experience to awaken our sympathy. But with the disease we have the remedy. The Psalm contains a prescription for a downcast soul, consisting of three ingredients, which we shall now consider in order.

The first is INQUIRY. *Why* art thou cast down? Religious despondency must have a cause; and if we can discover it in any case, the old proverb holds good, that a knowledge of the disease is half the cure. Many a man is in great spiritual darkness, without knowing, or being able to discover the reason. He has been trying to live rightly, so far as he knows. He has not neglected prayer nor the house of God, and yet God seems to have hidden His face; his peace is gone; his soul is full of harrowing doubts and suggestions—deep calling unto deep in one continuous tone of menace or of wailing. In such cases the question which most vexes a sincere soul is, "Is this state of mind a mark of God's displeasure, or not?" As we shall presently see, it *may* be, but again it may *not* be. For instance, Christians sometimes forget that they have *bodies;* and that the condition of their bodies has a good deal to do with the brightness or darkness of their spiritual moods; and now and then a man, through sheer ignorance, persists in some course of life, some habit of eating or drinking, which, by keeping his body in an unhealthful state, correspondingly lowers the tone of his spiritual life. Often the devil which torments him is one that goeth not out but by fasting. It is a good deal gained when the man has discovered this; when he has found that, by a little attention to his *lower* life, he can get out from among the waves and billows which go over him, and can climb up to the high grounds of spiritual peace and clear-seeing. Or the cause may lie deeper, in some mental disease—possibly an inherited one. You know the case of the poor hypochondriac poet, Cowper, who wrote :

> " Where is the blessedness I knew,
> When *first* I saw the Lord ? "

And again, in the very spirit of the fourth verse of this Psalm :

> " What peaceful hours I *once* enjoyed !
> How sweet their memory still !
> But they have left an aching void,
> The world can never fill."

Did you ever hear anything sadder than this ?—" Adam's approach to the tree of life, after he had sinned, was not more effectually prohibited by the flaming sword that turned every way, than mine to its great Antitype has been, now almost these thirteen years. For what reason it is that I am thus long excluded, if I am ever again to be admitted, is known to God only. If the ladder of Christian experience reaches, as I suppose it does, to the very presence of God, it has nevertheless its foot in the abyss. And if Paul stood, as no doubt he did, when he was caught up into the third heaven, on the topmost round of it, I have been standing and still stand on the lowest, in this thirteenth year that has passed since I descended." You see what hypochondria will do.

But then, on the other hand, the distress *may* arise from estrangement between man and God. One may be among the billows because he has voluntarily tempted them. Peter, when he went out and wept bitterly, was cast down and disquieted as he deserved to be. He had put himself by his cowardice and treachery among the black billows of remorse. And no Christian can expect bright outlooks, a clear sense of acceptance with God, a peaceful conscience, who is living in the habitual neglect of known duty, or in the habitual indulgence in known evil. Anything which, under such circumstances, seems like peace and joy in the Holy Ghost is a delusion. Such depressed spiritual states will be very likely to follow the neglect of *prayer* for instance. The road which leads *to* the closet is the road to hope and to praise. The road which leads *past* the closet leads down to the billows. Or, depression may come from the neglect of the public means of grace. If God's minister hung out a lamp for *your* feet and a light for *your* path on the day when, for your own pleasure, you stayed from the house of God, whose fault is it if you are bruised and sore from your fall into the trap which the light illumined, but which you were not there to see? Perhaps there was a time of refreshing from the presence of the Lord at that social meeting to which you did not *choose* to go; and you know what Thomas, the doubter, lost because he was not with the disciples when Jesus came.

Or the question, "Why art thou disquieted?" may open suggestions of another kind. If you cannot, on inquiry, discover that *sin* is at the bottom of your disquietude, it may occur to you that *God* has sent it. It is not unlike Him to disquiet those whom He loves sometimes, in the way of His discipline. You are in affliction, it may be, and in the despondency which affliction brings with it. Why art thou disquieted, my soul? God knew of this affliction, did He not? He could have averted it, could He not? Yes, and yet He suffered it to fall. If then He *in-*

tended it for thee, O Soul, why art thou disquieted? Thou art satisfied that the source of thy trouble is *divine;* is that something to be disquieted about? Or dost thou fear it will be more than thou canst bear? O reflect that the Father is the husbandman. He is pruning thee that thou mightest bring forth more fruit. Shall the knife in thy *Father's* hand cut off more than it is best thou shouldst lose for thine own growth's sake? Why art thou disquieted, my soul? Dost thou think thou art an exception in thy trial? Dost thou forget Him who was made perfect through suffering, and who was in all points tempted and tried like as thou art? Why art thou disquieted? Is it because thou canst not see the end thy God has in view in thy trial, or wilt thou forget that this "light affliction which is but for a moment, worketh out for thee a far more exceeding and eternal weight of glory"?[1]

Thus this "WHY" is one element of the Psalmist's prescription for spiritual despondency. Only, a man who is downcast must ask that question of his soul in good faith, meaning to get an answer if he can, and not sentimentally and insincerely, shutting his eyes to the revelation of what he more than suspects is at the root of his trouble. The only answer which will come back then from the questioned soul will be, "Thou knowest full well why I am cast down. Why dost thou mock God by asking why?"

But our prescription has a second ingredient, which is REMEMBRANCE; and in the Psalm we see this under two aspects; the Psalmist's remembrance of his own experi-

---

[1] 2 Corinthians iv. 17.

ence, and his remembrance of God's gracious dealing with others. In the fourth verse, his own experience recurs. "I am an unhappy exile now. My heart is heavy, and all God's billows have gone over me. But there was a happier time. I went with the multitude to the sanctuary. My heart was joyful, and my mouth was full of songs. At least let me not forget Thy benefits in the past. I will remember them and Thee with a thankful heart." Ah, how often we need the Psalmist's admonition to his own soul not to forget *all* God's benefits. Trouble, like a thick mist, has the power of exaggerating and distorting facts; and in the midst of it, we are very apt to forget that God has ever sent anything *but* trouble. We so readily say, "*All* Thy waves and Thy billows are gone over me." That is a mistake. Mr. Spurgeon's words are as true as they are beautiful: "*All* the breaking waves of Jehovah have passed over none but the Lord Jesus. There are griefs to which He makes His children strangers for His love's sake." But, on the other hand, He says that with Christ He will freely *give* us all things; and while we are so ready to say—"*All the waves* have gone over me," we do not say to our souls—"Forget not *all* His benefits." And I know no better cordial for a downcast soul than the recollection of God's mercies. They will crowd, at the summons of memory, thickly down to the very edge of to-day's trouble, like the cloud which followed the Israelites down to the marge of the Red Sea; and like that cloud will send light over the troubled waters through which lies the line of march. To-day's trouble will be lighter, and to-day's outlook more hopeful through the remembrance of the blessed past.

But this remembrance of the Psalmist also takes in God's dealings with His people. No one has such a range of history at his command as the believer who is in trouble; since the history of God's children is largely made up of trouble, and as largely of God's deliverances out of trouble. And the form which this truth takes here, while it is poetical, is at once instructive and beautiful. The scene of the Psalm is among the mountains on the east of the Jordan valley. From these mountains the spectator had unfolded to him a magnificent panorama of the Land of Promise. Lebanon, the sea of Galilee, the plain of Esdraelon, Carmel, the Mediterranean, the whole range of the mountains of Judah and of Ephraim, Bethlehem, and Jerusalem, could be seen from different standpoints. As to the traveller from the East, to Abraham and to Jacob, for example, coming from Mesopotamia, the first view of the promised inheritance burst upon the sight in descending these mountains, so, in later days, it was from these same heights that many an eye took its last look, through falling tears, at the familiar scenes of home and worship. The ridge was in a sense consecrated by the tears and sighs of exiles. David, in his flight from Absalom, Abner, driven by the Philistines, the captive Jews on their way to Babylon—each and all had turned ere they went down to "the great red plains of the East," or plunged for hiding amid the mountain defiles, to look their last upon the land of their love and pride. And yet just here, amid so many distressing associations, the exile or the captive might look off from the hill Mizar or from any other summit of the range, and recall enough of God's goodness to His people to fill him with wonder and love, and almost to make him forget his own trouble. How many displays of His power, how many visions of His beauty were associated with that very ridge. There was Mahanaim, "the two camps," where Jacob, afraid at the coming of Esau, had met the host of God, and had learned that there was another camp there beside his tents and flocks; that "the angel of the Lord encampeth round about them that fear Him and delivereth them."[1] There, in the deep bed of the Jabbok, he had wrestled with the Covenant Angel, and had won the crown of a Prince of God. From those heights Moses had beheld the Land of Promise, and Balaam had prophesied the future glory of Israel. There was Jordan, which had parted for the passage of the conquering people, and had held back its sweeping waters while the ark of God stood still in the river bed. There was Jericho, with the memories of the circling priests and of the falling ramparts:— the whole wondrous history of God's deliverances for Israel was spread out in panorama before the sorrowful eyes of the exile; and he might relieve his sorrow and fortify his spirit by the perusal of this record. So it is that in the sorrowful passages of Christian life, God often makes use of the memories of His goodness to strengthen and to encourage us. The height to which sorrow leads is rugged and storm-swept, but it often commands a wonderful retrospect. Sometimes a man is so engrossed with the pleasure and business of the present, that memory has no chance to do her work, and he is in danger of forgetting God's benefits altogether; and so God leads him away alone, whither he does not like to go, but where, cut off from the occupations of the present, he has opportunity to survey the rich and fruitful past, and to grow grateful amid his sorrow. Yea, often the very land of exile is the land of precious memories. More than one has found the very path where God has caused him to walk in tears, most fruitful in memories of blessing. At any rate, with such a history of God's salvation at our command, we cannot tread *any* path, however rough, but that we shall find footsteps there before us—memorials of God's deliverance on that very spot. Men of old have had their faith, their courage, their patience, tried sorely in the very places where *our* faith and courage and patience are tried; and their experience of God's saving goodness and power calls on us to remember that the God of salvation is the same, yesterday, to-day, and forever. It is worth noting how this element of remembrance was emphasized in all God's discipline of His ancient people; how often their history was rehearsed in their hearing; how, on every occasion of note, they were bidden to rear visible memorials like Jacob's stone at Bethel, or the cairn on the Jordan bank to commemorate the parting of the river, or the stone Eben-ezer set up by Samuel as a memorial of victory. And even in the very forms of address to God, this element comes in. "God of Abraham, of Isaac, of Jacob"—every such address, while it draws the thought of the worshipper to his Divine Helper, also reminds him of the men whom God has helped, and strengthens his faith by the memory of God's goodness and compassion in the past.

A few words, now, concerning the third ingredient of

the prescription, which is HOPE. "Hope thou in God, for I shall yet praise Him."

And notice, in the first place, that hope is to be *in God*. There is nothing like trouble to open a man's eyes to the need of a *personal* God. All the talk about God being an essence diffused through rocks, and trees, and waves, and all the various forms of nature, is worse than chaff to the soul that is cast down and disquieted by calamity or by sin. It is a very pleasing sentiment as one stands safely on the shore, that God is in those foaming, tossing billows; but when all the waves and billows are going over a man, he wants a God who is *apart* from the billows, and who rules the raging of the sea. In the midst of calamity, man's heart cries out for a Father in heaven. "What we want," says one who knew as much as any other man of the deep desolation of sorrow, is not *infinitude*, but a boundless ONE; not to feel that love is the *law* of the universe, but to feel One whose name is love; for else, if, in this world of order, there be no one in whose bosom that order is centred, and of whose being it is the expression, then order, affection, contrivance, wisdom, are only horrible abstractions, and we are in the dreary universe alone. It is a dark moment when the sense of that personality is lost; more terrible than the doubt of immortality."[1]

Then, too, the downcast soul must hope in *God*, and not in *change of circumstances*. There is a great deal of hope which rests *only* upon change of circumstances, and which does not touch God at all. A man is downcast,

---

[1] Frederick W. Robertson.

for instance, because he has lost his property ; but what hope he has, he gets out of the possibility that his prosperous days may return, and that he may be a rich man again. True hope, the Psalmist's hope, would say, " This loss is God's work ; I am God's child ; this is God's discipline ; through this He may be working out for me something far better than worldly prosperity. The best thing I have left, the thing to which I anchor my present and my future is—God is mine. This matter is all in God's hands, and whatever He may do with me or with my fortune, whether He give back my prosperity or not, I shall yet praise Him who is the health of my countenance and my God."

And, once more, this hope is a different thing from faith, while the operations of the two are nevertheless closely allied. God's people now and then get into just such places as the writer of this Psalm was in, when the waves and billows are going over them, and when faith does not *realize* the presence of God, and cannot *feel* it for the time. Then they cry, like Job, " Oh that I knew where I might find Him." When a physician gives to a sick man a remedy which for the time increases his distress, he does not *realize* nor *feel* that the work of restoration is going on ; and in the dark places of Christian experience through which God causes a man to pass in the course of His discipline, the man does not always realize that God is doing a beneficent work upon him, or *how* He is doing it. Then hope comes in. " If we hope for what we see not, then do we with patience wait for it."[1] Under such

---

[1] Romans viii. 25.

circumstances one is tempted to call out to God in his sorrow, " Why dost Thou deal with me thus ? " And the answer he gets is, " What I do thou knowest not now, but thou shalt know hereafter;"[1] so that we can only *hope* in God. Clouds and darkness are round about him ; he cannot see the light of God's countenance, but he knows the bright face is behind the cloud, and waits in confident hope that " the Lord will command His loving kindness in the daytime " and His song in the night.

Here, then, is God's own prescription for a downcast and disquieted soul. So many of these there are to-day, buffeting the stormy tides of business, torn away from much in which their hearts delighted, filled with dread of the uncertain future—to such the Psalm addresses itself, bidding you *inquire*, " Why art thou cast down ? " Perhaps you are *wrongfully* disquieted; perhaps because you were trusting too much to riches or to position ; perhaps because you have strayed from God, who ought to be your chief joy ; or, possibly, your disquietude is *His* call to you to come back to His side. At all events, it is worth while to find the cause if you can ; and in finding the cause you may find the remedy. It bids you not to forget gratitude in your sorrow. It bids you remember the wonderful mercies of God, and to strengthen your faith with the thought that He who has wrought so graciously for you and for His people in the past, will be your God forever ; your guide even unto death.[2] It bids you *hope*, never losing out of your mind the *disciplinary* purpose of God in all sorrow, and waiting in the confident expec-

---

[1] John xiii. 7.   [2] Psalm xlviii. 14.

tation that "these light afflictions, which are but for a moment," shall work for you "a far more exceeding and eternal weight of glory."[1] If not here, why then by and by. If the clouds do not disperse until the dark river be past, yet you may walk by God's voice though you see not His face; and in the land of eternal light you shall *forever* praise Him, who through all the changes of this mortal life is still YOUR GOD, and who shall be yours forever.

---

[1] 2 Corinthians iv. 17.

THE GATE TO THE CAVE.

PSALM LVII.

(1) Be gracious unto me, O God, be gracious unto me,
For in Thee hath my soul found refuge;
And in the shadow of Thy wings will I find refuge,
Until the destruction be overpast.

(2) I will call upon God Most High,
Upon the God who conferreth benefits upon me.

(3) He shall send from heaven and save me,
——Though he that would swallow me up hath reproached—
God shall send His loving kindness and His truth.

(4) As for my life—in the midst of lions must I lie,
(Among) those who are ready to devour, (even) the children of men,
Whose teeth are spears and arrows,
And their tongue a sharp sword.

(5) Be Thou exalted above the heavens, O God,
(And) Thy glory above all the earth.

(6) They prepared a net for my steps;
My soul was bowed down.
They digged before me a pit;
They fell into the midst thereof (themselves).

(7) My heart is steadfast, O God, my heart is steadfast;
I will sing and play (upon the harp).

(8) Awake up, my glory; awake harp, and lute;
I will wake the morning-dawn.

(9) I will praise Thee among the peoples, O Lord,
I will play unto Thee among the nations.

(10) For great unto the heavens is Thy loving kindness,
And unto the clouds Thy truth.

(11) Be Thou exalted above the heavens, O God,
(And) Thy glory above all the earth.

X.

THE GATE TO THE CAVE.

(7) " My heart is fixed, O God, my heart is fixed ; I will sing and give praise."—Psalm lvii.

THIS psalm is very strangely compounded. It is described in the title as the utterance of David when he fled from Saul and hid himself in the cave.[1] It is the cry of a man beset with trouble and danger; yet all through it, we are startled by sudden transitions from cries for help, and stories of wrong to cheerful expressions of hope and outbursts of praise. Thus it begins in the sad minor strain : " Be merciful unto me, O God, be merciful unto me : for my soul trusteth in Thee : yea, in the shadow of Thy wings will I make my refuge until these calamities be overpast. I will cry unto God Most High." Now there is a hint of better things : " Unto God who performeth all things for me." Now a change into a tone of bold, cheerful hope : " He shall send from heaven and save me from the reproach of him that would swallow me up. God shall send forth His mercy and His truth." Now into the minor key again : " They have prepared a net for my steps ; my soul is bowed down. They have digged a pit before me." And still another change, and this time into an exultant strain :

---

[1] 1 Samuel xxiii.

"My heart is fixed, O God, my heart is fixed: I will sing and give praise. Awake up, my glory: awake psaltery and harp: I myself will awake early."

This condition of hopefulness and of cheerful steadfastness in the midst of trouble is one of those things which always puzzle a mere man of the world, but which present no mystery to a soul which walks with God. But the fact goes much farther than cheerfulness in trouble. The word "*fixed*" literally means "*prepared*," "*fit*," "*ready*." "O God, my heart is prepared." Among the most uncongenial circumstances, in times and places most unsuited for worship or for praise, for composed thought and joyful communion, the Psalmist yet professes himself ready for worship and praise and communion. This would seem to indicate an *habitual* readiness of heart to turn to God under *all* circumstances. We might say that danger would *naturally* drive him to prayer, which would be true. That would enable us to understand the "Be merciful unto me," and "I will cry unto God;" but danger and sorrow do not habitually drive a man to *praise;* and when we hear him in such circumstances, saying—"I will sing and give praise," the only conclusion we can come to is that that man lives *habitually* in an atmosphere of faith and of heavenly communion, so that in *all* seasons his heart is *prepared* to wait on God. It is about this habitual preparation of heart that I wish to speak.

The *ideal* perfect Christian life would be a life in contact with God along its whole line. It would be *everywhere* and always in communion with God. God's will and God's love would fill and move in every inlet and curve of the life, as the ocean in its gulfs and creeks and round its promontories ; and upon this high plane, the general tenor of the life would be more even. There would be no struggles for the vision of God's face when His face should be constantly unveiled. There would be fewer, or, perhaps, *no* seasons of special communion with God, when the whole life should be one long communing with Him. The seer on Patmos, in his vision of the heavenly Jerusalem, saw no temple therein. There was no need of the special forms and occasions of worship where the spirit lived forever in the immediate presence of Christ.

It hardly needs to be said that we do not live in this condition, and that we do need certain special influences to recall our minds to heavenly things, to lift them into the atmosphere of rest and of devotion, and to keep them from drifting away into worldliness and sensuality. God has recognized the need and has met it. He has given the Sabbath with its rest from labor, He has given the sanctuary with its quickening influences, He has commended the season of special prayer, He has made prayer draw some of its inspiration and get some of its character from special facts, as for example, in *family* prayer ; He has instituted the sacraments to be formally, statedly, and decently observed, and thus has attached a certain spiritual power to occasions, of which He expects us to avail ourselves to the largest extent for the quickening of our religious life ; so that we are not justified in neglecting or despising these things because the perfect *ideal* of Christian living omits them. It may be true that, in a future day, we shall ask Him nothing, because the perfect oneness of the divine life and ours shall do away with the necessity of asking and receiving ; but it is true *now* that we are to ask and receive. There may be no temple in the heavenly Jerusalem; but on earth, it remains true that the Lord loveth the gates of Zion, and bids His people not forsake the assembling of themselves together.[1] It is true that by and by the disciples shall drink the new wine of the kingdom with Christ in heaven, or, in other words, shall exchange symbolic for personal communion; but none the less are we bidden now to assemble round His table, and to do this in remembrance of Him.

Moreover, we are not to ignore the spiritual power which attaches to stated religious occasions. We may say that, in a perfect state, religious experience would be much more level, that there would be no alternations of feeling, that the soul would habitually live in an atmosphere of holy joy and peace. That may be; though even in the perfect, ideal state, I am not sure that spiritual experience will be a dead level, or that there may not be exceptional heights of spiritual vision and ecstasy, rising even above the high table-land of *heavenly* life. Be that as it may, we are to accept the fact that these special religious occasions induce quickened feeling, and quickened spiritual perception. After you have been immersed in business and distracted all day with worldly cares, it would be strange indeed if the influence of the place of prayer should not lift you into a calmer region, and bring you into closer communion with Heaven. Even as the feeling of the disciples was more deep and intense on that evening when they gathered round the table in the upper chamber, when the sense of the approaching crisis was on

---

[1] Hebrews x. 25.

their hearts, and when every word and act of Christ took on a double impressiveness—even, I say, as their feeling was more intense than in their daily, ordinary intercourse with their Master — so in the sacrament, in which we more definitely recall those closing scenes, and read their meaning in the light of our own spiritual experience, and of the history of Christ's atoning work through all the Christian centuries — we may expect to have feeling heightened, and thought quickened, and perception clarified. Life is not *all* spiritual. The flesh lusteth against the spirit, and the continuous fight will issue in alternations, variations of the level of Christian joy and peace, depressions from which we must be raised by special influences, " unmannerly distractions," from which we need the closet and the sanctuary and the communion to recall us.

But, this being admitted, we are none the less to guard against the tendency to make our Christian life and experience, our Christian peace and restfulness centre in these occasions. We see this tendency breaking out in its grosser forms, in the cases of those who dissociate religion and morality ; in the devotee who leaves the confessional or the communion to begin a new series of debaucheries ; in one who formally abstains from certain amusements, or gayeties, or indulgences, and carefully frequents church during Lent, only to give up the rest of the year to unbounded worldliness ; in one whose thought detaches itself from business or from pleasure only at the time of communion, and who devotes himself for a week to special preparation for that event, and then drops back again into the sweeping tide of the world, and goes down with the current until another communion season.

These, I say, are grosser manifestations of this tendency. They do not indicate a fixed or prepared heart, but a heart which must be specially worked up to special preparation at definite intervals. There are subtler manifestations of this tendency. Sometimes I have been led to question whether this very service[1] does not reveal some of them.

Christ ordained the sacrament, but He ordained prayer also. The preaching of the word is as truly His institution as the sacrament of His passion and death. Fidelity to the observance of the sacrament is enjoined by Him, but so is fidelity to every other duty; and neither Christ nor His apostles anywhere emphasize fidelity to one observance to the neglect or disparagement of the others. If it be the duty of Christians to hear the word when it has special reference to the celebration of the communion, I cannot understand why it is less their duty to hear it when it bears upon other departments of Christian duty. If a devotional and tender spirit in the Church is desirable every two or three months on the eve of the sacrament, I do not understand why it should be less desirable every week, or how conscience can acquit a Christian for the neglect of the means instituted for fostering it.

Let us clearly understand, then, that all special occasions in the life of church or of individual—church services, stated preaching, social meetings, closet communing, sacraments—are aimed directly at our *ordinary* life : are designed to help us live that better. We are led up to these Pisgahs and Hermons of spiritual vision, to the end

---

[1] Preparatory lecture before communion.

that we may carry the power of these visions into life's common routine, to sanctify and to elevate that. These things are not an end unto themselves. Christ Himself withdrew to the mountains for high and solemn converse with God—a communing on which the imagination refuses to intrude—in order that He might be braced and inspired for the daily contact with commonplace minds, and with the wretchedness, filth and squalor, the disease, and ignorance, and bigotry to which so much of His life was employed in ministering. The disciples were not permitted to stay on the Transfiguration Mount, but that glorious vision would have failed of its main purpose if it had not strengthened and kindled their hearts for the hard mission for which they were chosen. These exceptional experiences in our lives are intended to foster in us that constantly prepared, fixed heart of which David here sings: the heart that shall be prepared for praise, and for trust, and for worship, not only while sitting in heavenly places, but also among lions, among them that are set on fire, when the net has been prepared for the steps and the soul is bowed down, amid the fret and worry of life, and on the dead level of daily duty and care.

It is a great thing to have a heart thus prepared, but it is not an impossible thing. If the Bible is to be believed, there have been men who *walked* with God. Paul says, " Our *conversation* is in heaven," [1] and that does not mean merely talking about heaven or hoping for heaven, but living habitually in a heavenly atmosphere, in which one is sensitive and responsive to every voice from heaven.

---

[1] Philippians iii. 21.

And you have met such persons: men who went vigorously about their business like other men; who seemed to be as much absorbed in it as other men, yet who never seemed to find it hard to slip into talk about heavenly things, and whose response to any suggestion of heaven or of divine truth was so quick and natural and unforced that you saw at once that the heart was *prepared*, and that God and Christ were the uppermost facts in their lives. And that prepared state of the heart settles a great many questions. There, for instance, is the question of Sabbath observance. You find persons who challenge its claim to be a day of religious worship and instruction. "It is a day of rest," they say. "Why should we mew ourselves up in church? Why should our thoughts be forced into religious channels? Why should we not spend the day in amusement?" A Sabbath thus observed under protest could scarcely be profitable; but that matter apart, the question is settled for a prepared heart by never being raised. When you have a holiday, you generally spend it in doing the thing most congenial to you. You hunt, or fish, or read, as you please. And similarly if God is a man's best friend, if his heart is charged with love to God, the day which relieves him from the distracting cares of business, will find him not only ready but eager to meet the Lord in the sanctuary. The opportunity of dwelling on the congenial truths of revelation will be eagerly embraced. It will not be a question of *duty* at all, but a leaping of the heart for very joy as it moves into the green pastures of the word. Such an one will rest, but he will rest in the Lord. A friend once said to me, "When I was a boy in my father's house, and we were singing at family worship or at other times, the chords of the piano, though no one struck the keys, would often vibrate so strongly as to startle us all. Only, if we happened to sing a little off the key—a little too high or too low—the instrument would be mute." And the ordinances of God's house—worship, praise, preaching, sacraments—are a good deal like that piano. If the heart is prepared, if the life is set in the key of love and faith, these things will respond most harmoniously and mightily. You know how it is sometimes, that a social meeting or a communion season seems to fill the whole soul with its gracious influence : when you are as sensitive and responsive to every thought and word as the aspen to the wind. Perhaps you thought that the service *in itself* was unusually interesting and impressive ; but often the impressiveness has grown out of the fact that you were in right relation to the service; that your heart was prepared, your devotional feeling set in the right key. We might very easily have more of such delightful seasons; the secret lies mainly in having a prepared heart; in maintaining the glow of faith and prayer in our daily walk ; in *keeping* our heart tender and susceptible to divine influences. If you come to the sermon or to the place of prayer without such preparation of heart, depending on the occasion to lift you bodily into a condition of sympathy with heavenly things, the chances are you will be disappointed. Most of the spiritual energy of the occasion will be expended in bringing you up to the point from which you ought to have started. Some of us remember the old-fashioned foot-stoves which our grandmothers used to take with them to church in the olden days. The reason why the stoves kept them comfortable in church, was because they put the fire in them before they left home, and fanned the fire in their walking or riding to the sanctuary; and that church will have the warmest and most sympathetic atmosphere in its Sabbath services and social meetings, where there is most godly living and prayer and meditation on the word in the daily experience of its members. The fire will be ready kindled in those prepared hearts when they reach the sanctuary, and a single breath of the spirit will set them in a glow. There is a difference in the way social meetings are conducted: one man is a better leader than another. There is a difference in sermons. A pastor may preach a good sermon one Sabbath and an inferior one the next; but, after all, the difference in the tone of religious services is not altogether explained by these variations; a part of the cause lies with the people. Scripture tells us of those to whom the word was preached faithfully and pungently, yet who were not profited thereby because they did not hear it with faith.[1] Isaiah's lips were touched with a coal from God's own altar, and yet, in sending him forth to his work, God said, " Go and tell this people, 'hear ye indeed but understand not; and see ye indeed but perceive not. Make the heart of this people fat, and make their ears heavy, and shut their eyes; lest they see with their eyes and hear with their ears, and understand with their heart, and convert and be healed.' "[2]

We need, then, to keep in mind clearly this thought— that religion in the ordinary life—*habitual* communion with

---

[1] Hebrews iv. 2.   [2] Isaiah vi. 9, 10.

God, daily abiding in the atmosphere of heaven—is the great end to which Christ and His apostles point us ; and that all special or exceptional religious agencies point that way, and have their chief value in fostering the condition which is described as having the conversation in heaven. It is right that we should look up and forward from the routine, or struggle, or distraction of our lives to these mounts of vision, with expectation and with longing; but it is also right and indispensable that we should look *from* the mountain-top down along the stretch of dusty, rocky road to which we must soon descend, and feel that the prime object of the blessed rest and clear revealing of the mountain is, that we may walk the more diligently and tranquilly and patiently on the road. Too often our lives are like buildings of two stories ; one on the ground, damp and cluttered with bales and boxes and household stuff, blackened with smoke and ringing with the clamor of business and of domestic life, and where we pass most of our time. The other, whither we climb on Sundays, perhaps once a week besides, possibly for a few minutes each day—a place where more of God's light comes in, where there is more quiet and less outward taint of sordidness, and where we have an outlook at the sky and beyond the limits of our daily round of domestic, or business, or other care, and get out of the reek of the lower story for the time. It is well that we do this so often ; well that we have a higher plane for our lives to walk on now and then ; but it might be better. Granting we must have the two stories, there is no reason why all the light and freshness should be confined to the chambers whither we go up to look at the heavens and to commune with God. Windows ought to be cut somewhere to let the light and warmth from above into that ground floor; and the breath of God ought to have some way of getting in there and lifting the dull atmosphere of care and worry. There will be a difference between the two stories, but it ought not to be so marked. Christ, with all His power and sweetness and refreshing, is willing to come down into our *common* life; to teach us how to make our "common task" "bring us daily nearer God;" and the seasons which we spend in the upper chambers ought to make us so in love with Christ's presence that we cannot do without it when we descend, but must have Him, as He desires to be, "with us *alway* even unto the end of the world." When He shall thus abide with us and we with Him, all our life, whether commonplace or sublime, will get its character from that abiding: business, domestic life, pleasure, all will fall into the key of His spirit, and he who thus walks with Him, will know, in the ready response of every detail of his life to Christ's touch, what the Psalmist meant when he said—"My heart is prepared."

"My heart is fixed." "Ah!" one will say, "My heart! There is just the trouble: that traitorous, rebellious heart; if I could only get it fixed and resting in God, then indeed it would be prepared for all things; but to-day it is at peace with God, the next day laden with the consciousness of sin. To-day it rejoices, to-morrow it will be in heaviness through manifold temptations; to-day it is hopeful and trustful, to-morrow it will, very likely, be racked with doubt; to-day I think it consecrated fully, to-morrow I may have reason to doubt whether it is consecrated at all."

I think there is comfort for you. Very probably you try to get out of this experience by renewing your consecrations at intervals, by making new and solemn vows and resolutions, by endeavoring by the act of your will to make a full surrender of self, hoping that some time you will do this so thoroughly that God will no longer withhold Himself, and you will be free. And you may be sure that if you persevere in that course, you will not get free. You will keep on alternating between light and darkness, defeat and victory. Your heart will not be fixed. But there *is* a way out. If you will stop studying your own consecrations, and your self surrenders, stop studying self so much, and begin to study *Christ*, you will find that way out. That is to say, if, instead of feeling that you have got to fight your way to confidence and peace and habitual victory over temptation by a series of self-offerings, you will just *receive* Christ, and let Him come in and do the *whole* work, you will find it done much better. *He* will crucify self in you much more effectively than you can. It is they that *receive* Him that have power given them to become sons of God.[1] If Christ shall possess you fully, self will go out as a matter of course. I am reminded just here of the words of a venerable minister[2] now in heaven; a giant in the pulpit, and a little child in the wisdom of Christian experience. "Deliverance, habitual joy in God, and victory over old habits and temptations came when I had become perfectly assured that God had freely given Himself to me. I do not mean until God had revealed Him-

---

[1] John i. 12.   [2] Rev. Dr. James, of Albany.

self in a personal manner, but until I had become practically convinced and settled in the doctrine that *the love of God was a fountain for humanity, free, in its fulness, to every one who desired it; that nothing at all was required to make it mine; that it was mine now by virtue of what Christ had done for me, to which nothing could be added by me.* Sin and the world are already conquered so far as that persuasion is rooted in you; hold fast to it, and in a little while, God's glory will be a constant, loving manifestation." It was not strange that his peace was like a river, not strange that his heart was prepared, so that, when he saw the approach of death, he could write to a friend : "No young girl ever felt a more delightful fluttering in the prospect of a European tour, than I feel in the prospect of soon seeing the Land of never withering flowers ; of seeing Christ and knowing Him and being known of Him."

You want to go with a prepared heart to the Lord's table. I do not know any better preparation than you will find in that single thought :—The love of God is free, in its fulness, to every one who desires it. Nothing is required to make it yours beyond your accepting it. It is yours now by virtue of what Christ has done for you, to which nothing can be added by you. If that is true, you can but say joyfully as you move towards the table which tells you this truth in symbol,—"I am a sinner, I am weak, I am fallible, I am unworthy, but the love of God is mine, and Christ the gift of His love is mine, and therefore Christ's table is mine. It is my Father who presides at the board, it is my Elder Brother who meets me there."

The Gate to the Cave.

You want a thought to feed your mind while you eat the bread and drink the cup. This thought will last you longer than the hour of communion. The love of God is free in its fulness; yours now by virtue of what Christ has done for you. Can any thought impart to you a higher joy? Can the hungriest soul desire aught else to satisfy it?

And the hour of communion will pass, and the time come round but too quickly when you must plunge again into life's busy routine. You will cast a glance down into the seething and turmoil, and you will shrink. You will turn back to the peaceful scenes of communion as to a mount where you would gladly build a tabernacle and stay until the day shall come for drinking the wine new in the heavenly kingdom. But that may not be. The world calls you, and you must go and do God's work in the world like a Christian man or woman. Take this with you from the table to prepare your heart. The love of God is free in its fulness to every one who desires it. It is yours by virtue of what Christ has done for you. That thought will give a new character to your life. That thought, once grasped and held, will show you how life is yours with Christ—no longer the wave which smites and drives you at will, but *mastered* by you, made to help you on to God, and to make you meet, through its vicissitudes and trials for a better inheritance with the saints in light.

> " Too soon we rise. The symbols disappear;
> The *feast*, though not the *love* is past and gone.
> The bread and wine remove, but THOU art here,
> Nearer than ever, still my Shield and Sun.

* * * * *

I know that deadly evils compass me,
    Dark perils threaten, yet I would not fear,
Nor poorly shrink, nor feebly turn to flee;
    Thou, O my Christ, art buckler, sword, and spear.
But see! The pillar-cloud is rising now,
    And moving onward through the desert night.
It beckons and I follow; for I know
    It leads me to the heritage of light." [1]

---

[1] Bonar.

THE GATE TO THE SEA.

PSALM LXXVII.

(19) Thy way was in the sea,
And Thy paths in the mighty waters,
And Thy footsteps were not known.
(20) Thou leddest Thy people like sheep
By the hand of Moses and Aaron.

XI.

THE GATE TO THE SEA.

PERHAPS no illustration of divine power was better adapted to impress a Hebrew mind than this. A God who could rule the sea, and make His own and His people's path through the midst of it, must be a mighty God. For we, made familiar with the sea by our reading, our travels, our scientific researches, our sports—to many of whom a sea voyage is a luxury—we can but faintly realize the dread which the ocean inspired in a Hebrew. It was a significant threat which Moses threw out in his address to the Israelites, that, if they should refuse obedience to God, they should be carried back to Egypt *in ships*.[1] They would have dreaded the conveyance as much as the bondage itself. The ocean was a fearful mystery, and neither science nor experience mitigated its terrors. You never find in Old Testament poetry any of those musings upon the beauty of the sea, any of those expressions of restfulness and delight in its contemplation, which so abound in the writings of modern poets. David's ideal of happy repose is not a *seaside* retreat, but a walk by *still* waters. It is when he wishes to picture trouble, grief, sore extremity, frightful rage, that he brings in the sea.

---

[1] Deuteronomy xxviii. 68.

"All Thy waves and Thy billows are gone over me. Deep calleth unto deep at the noise of Thy water-spouts."[1] "If it had not been the Lord who was on our side when men rose up against us, when their wrath was kindled against us, then the proud waters had gone over our soul."[2] The very extreme of disaster from which God is confidently appealed to as a refuge, is the carrying of the mountains into the midst of the sea. God is our refuge even *then;* "though the waters thereof roar and be troubled, though the mountains shake with the swelling thereof."[3]

And therefore it added greatly to the impressiveness of Israel's deliverance from bondage, that it was associated so wonderfully with that realm of mystery and terror; that God should have led them through the sea, in its most awful aspect, " in the depth of midnight, amidst the roar of the hurricane which caused the sea to go back, amidst a darkness lit up only by the broad glare of the lightning, as the Lord looked out of the thick darkness of the cloud."[4] With all the triumph and joy which accompanied the event, its *mysteriousness* was distinctly and awfully marked. The dividing of the sea was a mystery; the pillar of cloud and fire, which led them through the depths, was a strange, weird, awful guide. They moved *through* mystery, and *after* mystery, following One whose footsteps were not known.

Out of these facts there springs up for us not merely an impressive symbol, but a great practical truth ; the truth namely that those who follow God, follow a leader whose

---

[1] Psalm xlii. 7.
[2] Psalm cxxiv. 2–5.
[3] Psalm xlvi. 2, 3.
[4] Stanley, Jewish Church.

footsteps are not known; that, in other words, he who accepts the service of God accepts with it much which he cannot understand, finds himself constrained both to do and to suffer much for which he can see no reason, and to order his life after a plan of which his reason cannot take in the whole circumference. Mystery, in short, is bound up with God's revelation and dealing with the human race; and though he no longer cleaves the sea nor kindles pillars of fire, it remains as true for us as it was for Israel that His way lies through deep places, and that His footsteps are not known.

The pride of the human heart rebels against such an economy as this. It wants to understand just *how* God makes a passage through the sea; and insists on forcing its way into the heart of the cloudy pillar to see how it is made up; and only on these terms will it yield its reverence and obedience.

And yet a very little thought will expose the unreasonableness of human reason in this matter. Such talk and reason as though God purposely and arbitrarily thrust upon them an economy of darkness and confusion; as though, in mere wantonness, He set himself at work to puzzle them; as though He deliberately beclouded things which they have the *right* and the *ability* to understand; forgetting that the *ability* to comprehend God is *just what is wanting;* that the *infinite* God *must* be incomprehensible to a finite being *in the very nature of the case;* and that the plans and dealings of an infinite Being will naturally partake of His own infinitude, and be, therefore, on a scale transcending human understanding. Zophar put the case to Job, and rightly, as a matter of simple impossibility. "*Canst* thou by searching find out God? Canst thou find out the Almighty to perfection? It is high as heaven; what canst thou do? Deeper than hell; what canst thou know? The measure thereof is longer than the earth and broader than the sea."[1] Take a little lad of ten years, and put him into an assembly of statesmen discussing the gravest questions of diplomacy and international law, to carry documents and messages from one desk to another. In that assembly the lad has a definite place and a definite duty which he can understand and do. But suppose he should refuse to carry a paper of which he did not understand the meaning and bearing. Suppose he should throw up his position as page, on the ground that he was not made acquainted with the whole course of complicated negotiation carried on in that chamber. Would any sane man regard the boy as an injured being? Would any one think of reproaching those statesmen with unkindness or injustice? Would not the lad be simply laughed at? Even supposing that every man in the chamber were disposed to grant his ridiculous demand and to explain the business to him—*could* they do it? *Could* the child's mind grasp the destinies of nations? And yet, if this is absurd, what shall be said of a finite being, with his scanty knowledge, with his limited capacity, with his little range of experience, refusing allegiance to a God whose purposes comprehend eternity, and move in orbits vaster than his utmost reach of thought can even begin to conceive; in whose plan the countless details of all being in the eternity, past and future, are grouped and

---

[1] Job xi 7–9.

unified—what, I repeat, shall be said of the stupendous folly of a poor little man, the difference between whom and God is barely *shadowed* by the difference between a statesman and a babe, yet who refuses allegiance to God because he cannot, by searching, find out the Almighty to perfection?

And not only so, but on their own principles, such men would refuse, if they *could* understand God. The proudest of them would say, "Never will I bow the knee to aught less than the infinite." And yet, to go back to the illustration, if the discussions of that assembly of statesmen were such as could be thoroughly understood by a child, if he could mingle freely in their talk, and interchange ideas with them, men would say that the assembly was a farce, and that its members were unworthy to deal with such mighty questions; and the boy himself would cease to revere them. So, if I may thoroughly *know* God, I must cease to *worship* Him. I cannot *adore* what I can *measure*. If His plans are within my comprehension, they are finite. If there is nothing in God which I cannot find out by searching, then God is finite and is not God. He lets me feel the touch of His hand, He daily compasses me with His love, He draws sharply for me the great outlines of His character, He restrains and forms me by His law, He teaches me by His providence, guides me by His wisdom, upholds and saves me by His power. But while there is thus a side of revelation in contact with me and daily available for me, I must never forget that it is *only* a side; that God's revelation is not God, but, as it were, a line of light on the verge of a narrow horizon, beyond which lie depths and glories of Divine Being unconceived and inconceivable by the heart of man.

This mystery of God's being naturally extends itself, as has been hinted, to His dealings with men. It is no more to be expected that we can understand all these than that we can understand Him; and hence His way in the world's history has been very largely a way in the sea, marked by much mystery and darkness, beset with hard problems which we are quite as far from solving as were the men of Job's day. There is the great mystery of evil for instance. Why did God mark out His path right through this awful fact of sin? How did it come into the world? Why is it not swept away by a righteous and pure God? Why must the Church spring up from the blood of the martyrs? Why are such carnivals of blood and lust as that now in progress under the very eyes of Christian Europe, tolerated? Why must helpless women and innocent children suffer at the hands of the vile Turk? Why is not that loathsome blot on the map of Europe wiped out at a stroke? Why do good men suffer and bad men prosper?

Or take the instruments with which God has carried on His work among men, a work involving so much knowledge, delicacy, and tact. He led His people by the hand of Moses and Aaron; of Moses whose hasty presumption debarred him from the Promised Land; of Aaron the maker of the golden calf; by the hands of wily and selfish men like Jacob; of wild, fierce men like Samson; of men stained with murder and lust and effeminacy like David and Solomon. By Elijah the prophet of fire; by Thomas who doubted, and by Peter who denied. So, down through the history of the Church, the Church which, somehow, has been a power in the earth to keep alive faith in the hearts of men, which has won souls, and defended the truth in the face of death, yet with such a large mixture of passion, pride, worldliness, and vanity in its saints. And the Church of the present! Why we shall be texts to the Church of the future, as the Church of the past furnishes texts to us. If we shall be held up as examples for their imitation, let us be sure that we shall furnish abundance of warnings also. And yet God's footsteps move on through all this error, weakness, narrowness, lovelessness in the very Church itself. Still He continues to put the gospel treasure in earthen vessels; continues to commission imperfect, erring men, to train and guide human hearts and souls; and through all their blundering, evolves results which awaken the wonder of men, and the joy of heaven.

Individual experience, too, proclaims the same fact from every side. Look at any single life; your own, if you will, for you know that best, and tell me if God's way in it has not been as a way in the sea. Ah, he is a wise man among you who can go back and explain his life. Talk of mysteries! You need not go to the sea, nor to the rocks to find them. Enwrapped in each separate manhood and womanhood is a mystery of providence deeper and subtler than any that the sea holds in its bosom. Child of God, Christian, do you know how you became what you are to-day? How is it that you are something different from what you meant to be, not so great it may be, or it may be greater? Or do you know why, supposing you are or have what you desired, you were led to it by a road so different from that which you chose? Do you understand why God has put certain responsibilities upon you, the very ones from which you shrank, or why, on the other hand, He has assigned to others the duties you coveted? Or do you know why your goal of earthly good is still below the horizon, and why God keeps you plodding along the road? He has smitten you where you thought you did not deserve it. He has taken away from you the earthly help you seemed to need most; He has let seven troubles come together when you thought you had your hands full with one; you believe God has led you, and yet His footsteps are not known. And you are not alone in this; you are in good company—the noble army of Patriarchs, Prophets, Apostles—of all of them as of Israel on the night of the exodus, it might be said, "Thou leddest Thy people by the way of the sea, and Thy footsteps were not known." It was a curious way of bringing Israel into Egypt by bereaving Jacob. It was a strange beginning of their wonderful emigration—the finding of a Hebrew baby in the Nile rushes. The sheepfold was a strange place in which to look for a king, and a ruddy shepherd lad a singular candidate for royalty. The school of Hillel, and the Sanhedrim, did not seem likely to furnish an Apostle of a gospel which recognized neither Greek nor Jew, Circumcision nor Uncircumcision. Yet so it has been, and is. This element of mystery enters into the personal experience of God's people everywhere, and in all times. On each life God writes this comment: "My thoughts are not your thoughts, neither are your ways my ways."[1]

Accepting this fact, then, what are we to do with it?

---

[1] Isaiah lv. 8.

The Gate to the Sea. 189

We have seen that it is an essential fact of God's infinity, and an universal fact in the history of His dealings. If we deal with God at all we cannot evade it. What then? Shall we submit to it passively and sadly, as those who yield to the inevitable, and who stand chafing at a door which God will not open?

We can do better than that. There is nothing discouraging in this truth, unless we persist in viewing it apart from other truths; and no truth of Scripture was ever intended to be viewed in that way.

In the first place, we are not to conclude that because there is a mystery in God's dealings, they are therefore without a plan. The ancient Jew, as he looked upon the sea, saw nothing there which suggested life or order or good. It was to him, as we have seen, the type of all confusion, danger, and trouble—a mere tumbling, chaotic waste. Not so the modern student. To him the heaving ocean suggests law and organized life. Its expanse is mapped, its depth is plumbed, the conformation of its bottom is known, the law of its currents is determined, and its inhabitants are classified. So, in viewing the dealings of God, often so dark, and confused, and apparently aimless, we are always to remember that the confusion is in *us* and not in God's work; that God's counsel is not darkened because we are blind.

Again, we are not to conclude that this mystery of providence is the outgrowth of unkindness. Now and then you will hear a man reasoning on this wise: "If God were the benevolent being I have been taught to believe Him, surely he would make this thing a little clearer." That is very poor logic. The man of olden time, with his overwhelming sense of the mystery and terror of the sea, knew not the bountiful mercy which was veiled by that mystery. Likewise mystery on God's part does not imply cruelty. We become entirely used to certain invisible and mysterious influences in nature, and we never are disposed to question their utility and blessing because they are hidden from us. The various atmospheric influences and electric currents, for instance, nourish and quicken our life, yet the most ignorant man never thinks himself hardly treated because he does not know the secrets of the air. We carry within us a greater mystery than any providence of God, and yet we do not call God cruel because he does not reveal to us the secret of the soul's life. And if we accept these things as consistent with divine benevolence, why not accept others equally strange to us? Luther was once in earnest prayer over some matter of great moment, desiring to know the mind of God in it, and it seemed as though he heard God say to him, "I am not to be traced:" and some one, commenting on this, adds, "If God is not to be traced, He is to be *trusted.*"

The writer of this Psalm has evidently reached very satisfactory conclusions on this subject. He is in great trouble and darkness; he is tempted to doubt the goodness of the Lord; he asks, "Hath God forgotten to be gracious?" But he reaches into the cloud which veils the Divine dealings, and draws strength and comfort out of it. He says, "This is my infirmity, but I will remember the years of the right hand of the Most High;" those very years when He veiled himself in darkness, yet amid thunders and hurricane led His people through the dark and dreadful sea. "Thy way was in the sea, and Thy path

The Gate to the Sea. 191

in the great waters, and Thy footsteps were not known. Thou leddest Thy people like a flock."

And the secret of this confidence is revealed in the 13th verse, in the words, " Thy way, O God, is in the sanctuary ; " or, as the best interpreters now render it, " Thy way is *in holiness.*" Put these two thoughts together, and one explains the other. Thy way is in the sea, dark, mysterious, dreadful; but Thy way is in holiness ; in perfect wisdom inspired by perfect love, and therefore a way of truth, leading up through the darkness into the eternal light. No matter how strange the way, if it be a way of holiness. What kind of a way that is Isaiah tells us.[1] It is a *clean* way : " the unclean shall not pass over it." It is a *plain* way for the trusting spirit : "The wayfaring men, though fools, shall not err therein." It is a *safe* way : "'No ravenous beast shall go up thereon." It is a way *for redeemed men,* redeemed from the world's economy of sight and sense, and translated into the kingdom and life of faith : they shall walk there, yea though it lie through the midst of the sea, with songs in the night and with everlasting joy upon their heads. No matter how deep the mystery, provided God's holiness is behind it. If any one less than God invite us to follow him into the dark, we may rightly tremble ; but if He leadeth His own people like a flock, what matters it by what ways ? So long as holiness leads, Asaph and Paul may unite in saying " We know that all things work together for good to them that love God, to them who are the called according to *His* purpose ; "[2] not their own purpose. If God calls us

---

[1] xxxv. 8–10.   [2] Romans viii. 28.

to fulfil His purpose, we ought to expect that He will lead us in His way, and, best of all, to His goal; and His goal is—"To be conformed to the image of His Son;"[1] but we shall not be that, until we see Him as He is; and that will not be here, but after the sea shall have been passed and there shall be no more sea.

"Thou leddest Thy people." The whole philosophy of life is here, here for us no less than for Israel. If we think we need some other theory of living because the Israelites were only poor slaves, and we intelligent nineteenth century Christians (or so we fancy), we are greatly mistaken. After all these centuries, God has nothing to add to this, that men let Him lead them, in His own way, through the sea if so He will it. The true philosophy of life, I repeat, is summed up here, in *simply following God.* Over the Apennines there is a wonderful railroad, on which, in a space of less than seventy miles, one passes through forty-three tunnels, some of them of very great length. The road is full of magnificent outlooks, but every few moments you go plunging into a tunnel. And certainly the traveller over this road would show his good sense by sitting still and being carried along the line of the rail; and not by getting out at the first station, and striking into the mountains to find another path, because he did not like the tunnels. He would be almost sure to be lost and to starve to death. The road has been built to carry him to his destination by the shortest way, and he will get there more quickly and safely through the tunnels than in any other way. O, if we could only believe the

---

[1] Romans viii. 29.

same thing of God's way! We want to build our own road, all out in the light; and the consequence is, it is much less direct than God's, and much more dangerous, and we cannot bring it out where we wish. God's way lies through the tunnels, long ones often, but it is the best road, the safest road: we shall reach the end most surely and quickly by it. And remember, it is not all tunnels either: in the region of the high rocks, where the tunnels are needed, are the most glorious prospects. If God's way is partly in darkness, the light places are full of beauty, commanding such outlooks of mercy and love as ought to reconcile us to the intervals of darkness.

I do not say that we ought not to make plans, nor to try to carry them out. Every earnest man will do that: only there is wisdom in holding our plans loosely, and subject to God's modification. Too often we are fettered by our plans: our minds are bent on carrying out our life along those lines, and when God proceeds to change those lines, they are so rigid that there is a good deal of friction and pain attending the change. A plan assumes a future, and involves forecast; and forecast is just the point where we are weakest, and the future the very thing about which we are most uncertain. Therefore, as a matter of ordinary probability, our plans will change: it is not to be supposed that we shall forecast the same things which Infinite Wisdom will forecast for us. It is wisdom to accept this fact, especially since we see it constantly illustrated in experience. I doubt if many men's success lies in the line they had marked out: often it lies in something running parallel with what they call their main work, in something which they style incidental; but the future proves that the power of their life centred in the incidental and not in the main work. A man, for instance, goes into a country town to pass a few months. Perhaps he is a learned man ; perhaps an eloquent man ; perhaps he has written books, or swayed multitudes from the platform, and has become accustomed to associate his efficiency with great efforts like these. And he probably thinks very little of his occasional contact with the people of that quiet town. He goes into their homes, a Christian gentleman, winning their respect and confidence and admiration by his bright, intelligent talk, and his Christian courtesy, and he goes away never perhaps dreaming that those few months of such intercourse may have wrought more than all his books and lectures. The trouble is that when such a man is laid aside from his greater work, and compelled to accept such desultory work, he is apt to rebel. His plan of life was laid out on what seemed to him the longer lines, and his pride is hurt when God lays it out on what appears to be a smaller scale. Well for him if he lets God lead him. We are apt to provide for the expansion of our plans, but not for shrinkage ; and he is the wise man who humbly follows God's leading ; who, though his road seems to lie straight and broad before him, out into wide domains of usefulness, happiness, and power, yet when God suddenly turns down some by-path, full of windings, leading he does not dream whither, obediently and cheerfully follows, content to go in dark and crooked ways with God, rather than on the widest path without him. I remember once, in Italy, climbing a mountain up which a broad, fine carriage road led almost to the summit ; but there the road suddenly ceased, and nothing appeared but a narrow foot-path leading round the shoulder of the mountain, and that soon dwindled into a sheep-track : and the sun beat down with terrible power, and the way was rough, and more than once I was tempted to go back ; but never shall I forget the vision which burst upon me as at last I reached the end of the narrow way : it repaid all the toil. So, I say, do not be afraid of the narrow way if God turns you into it. The great thing is that HE lead you ; and if HE lead, even though His footsteps are not known, you know that His way is in holiness, and ends at last in eternal good.

THE GATE TO GOD'S ACRE.

PSALM XC.

(1) Lord, Thou hast been our dwelling-place
   In all generations.
(2) Before the mountains were brought forth,
   Or ever Thou gavest birth to the earth and the world,
   Yea, from everlasting to everlasting Thou art God.
(3) Thou turnest frail men to dust,
   And Thou sayest ; ' Return, ye children of men.'
(4) For a thousand years in Thy sight
   Are (but) as yesterday, when it passeth,
   And as a watch in the night.
(5) Thou sweepest them away (as with a flood) ; they are (as)
      a sleep in the morning : [1]
   They are as grass which springeth afresh :
(6) In the morning it flourisheth and springeth afresh,
   In the evening it is cut down and withereth.
(7) For we have been consumed by thine anger,
   And by Thy fury have we been terrified ;
(8) Thou hast set our iniquities before Thee,
   Our secret (sins) in the light of Thy countenance.
(9) For all our days are passed away in Thy wrath,
   We have spent our years as a thought :
(10) The days of our years are threescore years and ten,
   Or (perchance) by reason of much strength, fourscore
      years ;
   And their pride is (but) labor and vanity,
   For it passeth swiftly, and we have fled away.
(11) Who knoweth the power of Thine anger,
   And Thy wrath according to the fear that is due unto
      Thee ?
(12) So teach us to number our days,
   That we may gain a heart of wisdom.
(13) Return, O Jehovah !—How long ?—
   And let it repent Thee concerning Thy servants.
(14) O satisfy us in the morning with Thy loving-kindness,
   That we may sing for joy and be glad all our days.
(15) Make us glad according to the days wherein Thou hast
      afflicted us,
   The years wherein we have seen evil.
(16) Let Thy work appear unto Thy servants,
   And Thy majesty upon their children.
(17) And let the graciousness of Jehovah our God be upon
      us ;
   And the work of our hands do Thou establish upon us ;
   Yea, the work of our hands establish Thou it.

---

[1] I have given Hupfeld's rendering of this passage, instead of Perowne's. So also Alexander.

XII.

THE GATE TO GOD'S ACRE.

LET your thoughts go back to the wilderness of the wanderings, where, for nearly forty years, the Israelites have been working out the terrible curse pronounced on them for their murmuring and rebellion. To Moses, as he gazed upon the scene, with its purple mountains, its deeply cut, narrow valleys, and the huts of the people clustering about the tabernacle, its suggestions and memories must be well nigh overpowering. Let us put ourselves, if we can, in the place of one whose life had been largely given to the guidance of this people, and who bore them upon his heart as his daily care ; and try to conceive the overwhelming power of this single thought—a whole people dying out in this lonely, rocky camp ; a nation waiting here in these solitudes until their fathers shall all have passed away under God's curse. And this was but one of many such thoughts which must have crowded on the mind of the man of God. There was his own history. First the bulrush ark, then the royal palace, then the quiet years in the mountain solitudes among the sheep, then back to face an angry king, and to wield the rod of divine vengeance over his empire, then the work for which all his past life had been a preparation, the endless, wearying duties of the leader and lawgiver of a slave population entering upon the inheritance of freedom : and then, as he looked forward, no more rest on earth : no dwelling for him among the sunny corn-lands and vineyards of the Promised Land. He too had sinned and he should not enter in. Forty years ! What years of change, of care, of decaying and renewed life, of tried patience :—and yet they were gone like a dream, and the new generation was stirring with the hope of the rest in the new land. Death, change, homelessness, human insignificance and frailty, these were the stories told by the lonely booths, the playing children, and his own whitened locks. What words would come more naturally to his lips under the burden of such thoughts, than these : " Lord, Thou hast been our dwelling-place in all generations. Ere these stern, purple mountains reared their heads, yea, ere the solid earth out of which they rise was created, from everlasting to everlasting, Thou art, O God."

It is the oldest of stories, sung in this oldest of Psalms ; of human weakness, turning in dismay from the change and decay about it, to find refuge in the eternity of God. The Psalm belongs to the nineteenth century no less than to Moses' time. It deals with universal, and not with temporary and local truths. Let us not be repelled from it because its undertone is sad and solemn ; for its lesson is wholesome if sad, bracing if bitter, and leading up to conclusions full of comfort and rest.

We cannot fail to notice how, at the very introduction of this sacred poem, we are confronted with a theological truth, dogmatically stated : and, in the general prevalence of the prejudice against all that is supposed to be conveyed by such words as dogma, doctrine, and theology, it will do

Bible-readers no harm to be reminded how much of all three there is in the Scriptures, underlying even its poems and allegories. The issue between doctrine and living, between theology and religion, is often raised out of a misunderstanding of terms: since there is no life-truth (so called) which does not rest on a doctrine, and no truth of religion, which does not belong equally to theology. The fact that a truth is a part of a theologic system does not affect its value any more than the healing qualities of a familiar field-plant are destroyed by its classification in a botanical treatise.

Look now at this Psalm, and observe that it sets out with the definite statement of a theologic doctrine, no less so because the form of statement is poetic;—the doctrine of THE ETERNITY OF GOD. And here we may gain some idea of the way in which the Bible teaches theology. This doctrine, for instance, is well adapted to call out theologic musing. Set the mind at work on this simple thought, *God is eternal*, and how the vast theme absorbs and leads it captive. How thought struggles with the problem of existence without beginning and without end. But the Bible never leads us so long in that direction, as to suffer us to become unconscious of our own spiritual condition. It furnishes abundance of themes adapted to excite musing and speculation, but it never suffers these musings to be an end unto themselves. The attributes of God, omniscience, omnipotence, justice, immutability, are not set forth merely as a pageant to excite wonder and awe. However Inspiration may kindle over them into poetic rapture, it is not long ere it begins to set them forth in their relations to the conscience and to the life. If it portrays the glory of

God in the starry heavens, it turns naturally to the perfection of the moral law as illustrated by the natural law.[1] If it kindles at the thought of the protecting tenderness of divine love, in almost the next breath it puts a prayer upon the reader's lips, laden with confession of helplessness, and with desire for the shelter of the wings of love.[2] The grandest portraitures, the most glowing statements of abstract truth, bear on their face a design to affect man's moral susceptibilities, to call out his love and homage, to foster his loyalty, to make him rejoice in moral order, and order his steps in the Divine Word.

In this Psalm, therefore, we are not suffered to waste time in the attempt to comprehend the abstract truth of God's eternity. The truth itself is plainly shown to have a practical bearing upon our mortal life, and this is the chief end for which it is presented. We are lifted for the moment, in order that we may descend; suffered to grasp a few of the treasures of the Divine Glory, that we may carry them back to glorify our earthly life.

Thus, in the first place, this splendid thought of the divine eternity is made to touch the shifting and inconstant character of our earthly state, by the single word "dwelling place." "Lord, a home hast Thou been to us, in generation and generation." We have seen with what relief Moses turned from the thought of the desert wanderings of the Israelites, to that of an abiding dwelling-place in God; and Paul puts himself in the same attitude when he says to the Corinthians, "For we know that if our earthly house of this *tabernacle* (or tent) were dissolved,

---

[1] Psalm xix.   [2] Psalm xvii. 7, 8.

we have a *building* of God, a house not made with hands, eternal in the heavens."[1] Now first this truth of God's eternity assumes a real interest to us. What matters it to me that God is eternal, if He be only the Epicurean's God, sitting aloof in eternal bliss and splendor, and letting time and change work their will with me and mine? But now God's eternity opens itself to my needs. I am a wanderer on earth, there is an eternal home for me : I am weary, there is eternal rest for me ; I am sick of confusion and change, there is eternal abiding in Him who is the same, yesterday, to-day and forever, and only a change "into the same image from glory to glory."[2] The eternity of God puts itself at my disposal to change my broken and transient communion with Him into eternal, confidential fellowship with Him ; to give me, for occasional glimpses of His face, the everlasting vision of the King in His beauty : to renew eternally the sweet Christian kinships and friendships which have passed away like a blessed dream, and left a long heartache behind. "An eternal home!" Often, as you walk through the halls of the Vatican, you may read these words on the tablets brought thither from the tombs of the heathen dead ; but the words freeze the heart as you read in them the utterance, not of hope, but of despair. *This* is the eternal home; this gloomy catacomb, this marble coffin. Better Moses amid the rocks of the desert, and the fragile huts of the long wandering tribes, with faith beholding an eternal home in the eternal God, than the Roman Patrician, turning from his city of palaces to confront nothing but a charnel-house.

---

[1] 2 Corinthians v. 1. [2] 2 Corinthians iii. 18.

But a correct view of the eternity of God conveys warning as well as comfort. The more it is studied, the stronger is the contrast into which it throws the brevity and uncertainty of human life. From this brevity and uncertainty we look up for refuge : from the refuge we look down upon human life with a deepened sense of its insignificance. This is the thought carried on in the next four verses of the Psalm ; for

1st.—The eternal power of God convicts us of *helplessness*. Notice the sharp contrast. " From everlasting to everlasting, O God," Thy life is self-sustained—in Thine own power : man's life, that gift in which he so exults and on which he presumes to play "such fantastic tricks before high heaven,"—that which flowers out in his pride and high endeavor, in his ambitions, plans, and grand enterprises, is a thing so little in his power, that Thou turnest him even unto the finest dust with a word ; and, with another word,—" Return, ye children of men "—callest others into being to fill his place.

2d.—The eternal being of God is used to convict us of *delusion*. We measure life by false standards. The Psalm brings us back to the true rule of measurement. " A thousand years, in Thy sight, are but as yesterday when it is past, and as a watch in the night. Teach us to number our days by Thy standard, that we may be wise." That old delusion, older than Moses, is woven into man's very nature, and is fed and flattered with every gilded cheat that his fancy can devise ; the delusion which leads him to think seventy years a long time. What need to dwell on a theme so trite, were it not that the delusion shows itself still so fruitful in mischief? Still the evil servant saith, " My Lord delayeth His coming," [1] and begins to eat and drink with the drunken, and to beat his fellow-servants. Still the master of the house comes suddenly, and finds the trusted servant with ungirded loins and extinguished lamp. Still men waste the hours, and delay repentance, and persist in rebellion, and at the bottom of all is this old cheat—life is long, there is time enough ; and notwithstanding all the denials repeated and emphasized by the swiftly passing generations, and by the daily growing cities of the dead, we still have need that Moses call to us out of the desert, and tell us that even the patriarchs' lives of centuries are represented to God's eye by a vanished yesterday, or a brief night-watch. What life is long, measured by an eternal standard? Well said Bengel, "As to a rich man, a thousand pounds are as a penny, so to God, a thousand years are as a day." Evidently we are poor reckoners when life is a factor of the problem. We need eternal wisdom to teach us to number our days, so as to apply our hearts unto wisdom.

These suggestions are enforced by the figures which follow. They will bear study : for they are not the mere overflowings of the poet's imagination. Each of them sets forth a truth of its own. There is, first, the fact that man passes swiftly from life. "Thou carriest them away as with a flood." And here let us try to get before us the picture which Moses had in mind, without which the saying will lose much of its force. He stood, as we have seen, in the desert, amid mountains penetrated by deep and narrow valleys, and he knew what a mountain torrent

---

[1] Matthew xxiv. 48.

was in those pent up defiles—a boiling, roaring flood, filling a valley sometimes to the depth of four hundred feet, carrying down huge boulders of rock as though they were so many pebbles, and sweeping whole families to destruction. Remember that a single thunder-storm, with a heavy shower of rain, falling on the naked granite mountains, is sufficient to convert a dry and level valley into a roaring river in a few short hours, and you have some faint idea of the intensity with which the swiftness of man's passage from time to eternity appealed to the mind of Moses. "Thou carriest men away from life, as a mountain torrent, rising in an hour, sweeps away the frail hut that man has built."

Take the next figure: and to the same thought of the swift passage of life, we have added that of its unsubstantial, unreal character, and of man's unconsciousness of its passage. Punctuate the fifth verse so as to read, "They are as a sleep in the morning." We lie down and wake, hours have passed, we know not how, yet the interval has been filled with dreams. We have been busy, we have achieved great triumphs, we have made long journeys, we have happily escaped from old troubles; but as the morning dawns, and we spring up at the rising of the sun to face life's actual work again, how dim and distant and unreal appear all these visions of the night. The success is not achieved, the old trouble not escaped. Perhaps we have overslept ourselves, and we are surprised and angry to find how much time sleep has stolen from us, while it has been beguiling us with dreams. Is it not a common experience, when a birthday or an anniversary comes to us like a waking hour, that we are startled to find how old we are, how little we have done, how many plans we must abandon, and wonder what has become of the time, and why that work which has kept our hand so busy and our brain so fretted, seems such a little unreal thing after all? "Surely every man walketh in a vain shew; surely they are disquieted in vain."[1] And when we shall have awaked in God's likeness, to see no more "through a glass, darkly," but "as we are seen," and to "know as we are known,"[2] we shall realize what we have so often sung together on earth,

"This life's a dream, an empty show."

Again, look at the third image: the grass which flourisheth in the morning and is cut down at evening. Here still is the old key-note—the quick passing of the life; but with a new thought, namely, how the beauty and strength and aspiration of life are disregarded in the swift flight of time. The grass may be taken here as the representative of vegetation generally; of something which is sown or planted with a view to future beauty or use; which struggles ever more into the light, and takes on colors, and blooms; yet what cares the mower for the beauty of a million of prairie-flowers? Human life is full of plans and ambitions ever growing toward something, rejoicing in beauty or looking forward to fruitfulness, and yet it is a familiar subject of comment how little time the best man is allowed to work out his plans. Just as he is ready to do the best work of his life, with his gathered experience and matured power, the blow falls, and the voice of God says, "return unto the dust."

---

[1] Psalm xxxix. 6.   [2] 1 Corinthians xiii. 12.

It is *cut down*. Why this strong expression, as if it were not left to wither of itself, but were destroyed by violence?

The question marks the transition to the next portion of the Psalm, embraced in the next four verses. This matter of brief life and swift death is a mystery, is it also an *accident?* Man does not always die by violence, often he lives longer than he can serve society, and passes away by what is called a *natural* death, and yet he is described as cut down. Already in the Psalm we have had a hint of a power and will behind this mystery of death. It is not said, man returns to dust, but "Thou turnest him;" and these four verses now bring out clearly the theme of which only single chords have been struck, this namely, *death is a cutting off, because of God's wrath against sin.* Listen! "We fail in Thine anger, in Thy wrath are we affrighted. Thou hast set our iniquities before Thee, our secret sins in the light of Thy countenance. For all our days are gone in Thine anger, we consume our years like a thought."

Man, therefore, is not here represented as *unfortunate*, but as *guilty*. Not as the victim of accident, but as the subject of punishment. The Bible, as some one remarks, throws the blame of death on man himself. And here again we have our poet teaching theology. Paul will take the thought out of its poetical form, and put it for you in set and logical phrase. "As by one man sin entered into the world, and death by sin, and so death passed upon all men, for that all sinned."[1]

---

[1] Romans v. 12.

And so the Bible wastes no time in sentimental condolence over the brevity of life and the swift coming of death. It is a fact to be dealt with, and not merely bemoaned. When the dweller in the mountain valley sees the water beginning to pour down along the dry channels, that is not the time for him to sit down and mourn that fate has led him to plant his home in such a spot. The devouring flood flows faster than his tears, and he must be up quickly and away to the high lands. The Bible speaks to man as to one that must be saved. "Thou art a sinner, O man! Thou art swept away like a flood because of sin. Thou art frightened because death draws nigh. Thou mayst well be frightened, but not at death. That which is behind death, that which propels it so swiftly and resistlessly is more terrible than death, the wrath of a holy God against sin." God has no easy good-nature or false tenderness which lead Him to conceal the terrors of sin. It is the Comforter who convinces of sin and of judgment.[1] His face beams with tenderness upon man, His voice calls him to find his home and his rest in the eternal God, but the very brightness of His face which lights up the way to eternal rest, brings out with terrible distinctness the outlines of human iniquity, and the secret sins which lurk in the deepest heart.

And it is interesting to see how, in this old Psalm, the same low views of this subject are recognized and censured, which characterize a large class of modern religionists. "Who knoweth the power of Thine anger?" "Who knoweth Thy wrath as becomes those that fear Thee?"

---

[1] John xvi. 7, 8.

Then as now, men were prone to say, "Man is to be pitied: man is the victim of circumstances: man is not guilty, but unfortunate: man is not depraved, but fettered: man deserves not punishment, but compassion: sin is no ground for wrath, but for tolerance." True it is that the Bible is an evangel of love and pardon and compassion: true that God knoweth our frame and remembereth that we are dust: true that "like as a father pitieth his children, so the Lord pitieth them that fear him;"[1] but also true that the Bible, from beginning to end, blazes like Sinai with God's hatred of sin, resounds with warnings of man's danger from sin, and sets forth as in letters of fire that man is responsible for sin, and liable to its penalties: true that History and Prophecy and Psalm and Gospel and Epistle are grouped round one definite purpose, to save him from the power, dominion, and consequences of sin. In view of these terrible facts, and of men's persistent blindness to the power of God's anger then as now, is it strange that Moses prayed, is there not good cause for *us* to pray, "Teach us to number our days?" Teach us how short our life is: teach us the true meaning of its brevity, as a punishment and not as an unhappy accident: teach us how we may use its brief hours to escape the consequences of God's wrath: teach us to number our days, until, as Thy humble pupils we bring a heavenly wisdom to bear upon the conduct of our lives.

The remaining five verses bring us back to the starting

---

[1] Psalms ciii. 13.

point of the Psalm. Whither should these contemplations of human mortality as related to sin, and of divine wrath against sin, cause us to turn but to God, our eternal home? Whither shall a sinful, short-lived man flee, but to a holy and eternal God? What can he say amid the gathering sadness of his swift-going days, amid the maze of his sins and infirmities, in his terror at the oncoming judgment—what but this, "Lord THOU art our dwelling-place in all generations?" Thither turns the prayer of these last five verses, and turns with hope and confidence. Man is the subject of God's wrath, but there is mercy with Him to satisfy him who flees from the wrath to come. Man is a pilgrim and a stranger, with no continuing city, but there is gladness and rejoicing in God for all his brief days. Man's beauty consumes as the moth, but "the beauty of the Lord our God" shall be upon him, and that beauty is immortal, untouched by time and change. Man's work is fragmentary, his plans often disconcerted, his grandest enterprises nipped in the bud by death, but God's touch upon human work imparts to it the fixedness of eternity; and if He establish the work of our hands, it shall abide though the world pass away and the lust thereof. He will make good the sufferings of sin by the joys of Holiness. Glory, beauty, establishment. A strange ending of this wail from the desert; and yet not strange in the gospel light in which we read it to-day. It is only the prophecy of the saved man's triumph over mortality and sin and death: of the victim of the down-sweeping flood snatched from its fury, and landed safely in the eternal dwelling-place in "the everlasting arms:" of the mown grass garnered, of the sleeper awaking, satisfied, in God's likeness. It is the foreshadowing of that blessed story of the wandering son brought home at last, and seated at the Father's table to go no more out forever.

THE GATE TO REST.

PSALM CXVI.

(7) Return unto thy rest, O my soul, for the Lord hath dealt bountifully with thee.

XIII.

THE GATE TO REST.

THIS Psalm is an expression of thanksgiving for deliverance from some great trouble. The trouble is set forth in very strong language. "The sorrows of death compassed me, and the pains of hell gat hold upon me : I found trouble and sorrow." The deliverance is referred directly to God. "He hath heard my voice and my supplications. I was brought low and He helped me. Thou hast delivered my soul from death, mine eyes from tears and my feet from falling." And, thus satisfied that he owes his deliverance to God, the Psalmist encourages his own soul to be tranquil once more. Thou hast been disturbed, tormented with the sorrows of death. Thy rest has been rudely broken. But God hath delivered thee, return unto thy rest, O my soul.

We cannot doubt where that soul's point of rest would be found. It simply goes back to God who has dealt bountifully, and rests in Him. Rests *lovingly ;* "I love the Lord because He hath heard my voice :" rests *obediently ;* "I will walk before the Lord in the land of the living :" rests *adoringly ;* "I will take the cup of salvation and call upon the name of the Lord :" rests *thankfully ;* "I will offer to Thee the sacrifice of thanksgiving :" rests *believingly ;* "I believed, therefore have I spoken." God is to that soul the permanent centre of love, obedience, adoration, thanksgiving, and faith.

This idea of rest in God, is in some sense a very familiar one to our Christian thought. It may be called, indeed, one of our staple ideas. It cannot be too familiar; but to be fully available it wants to be studied on all sides, and penetrated to its very core. The deeper we get into it, so far from finding ourselves in a region of speculation and abstruse philosophy, we shall find ourselves closer to truths which touch our life and thinking at vital practical points. What I have to say concerns not so much our attitude of restful faith, as it does God Himself as the centre of our rest; and if our faith has perchance in any way strayed from its resting point, perhaps these contemplations may help to draw it back.

Possibly we have come to think it unnecessary for us ever to inquire into the nature of our belief in God. We say, "*Of course* we believe in God." God is a fixed, unalterable fact in our religious consciousness: God is taken for granted by us in our thinking and doing: the belief in God has become so habitual that it is in some sense unconscious: we should as soon think of going down every month to examine the foundations of the house we live in. Well, my question is, whether it may not be desirable to go down now and then to this foundation truth, God? Whether it may not be well to bring it distinctly into our consciousness? Such a thing might be as a right foundation-stone wrongly laid. Probably none of us doubts the existence of God; probably all of us acknowledge Him as our Creator; probably most of us pay God some formal, stated recognition at least; and yet all this does not make it superfluous for us to examine the practical relation of the idea of God to our minds. What is God to us? How does He lie in our thought? How does the thought of God bear upon us? What does it do for us? How much does it restrain us? It has a resting-place in our souls, how much do we rest on it? What do we lay upon it and refer to it? For what does it stand as respects our views of our origin, our conduct, our destiny? It is just possible that, after prosecuting such an inquiry, we may find that God is, after all, much less to us than we have been used to think. We may find that there are certain points where we do not practically recognize His contact with our lives, where perhaps we rather avoid contact with Him. We may find that God is merely assumed by us to be somewhere *back of* our lives, in the dark, in a region of abstractions, instead of being a realized fact *in* our lives; that God, in short, is practically, little more than an idea, or a gigantic phantom looming dimly up through the mists and confusions of this earthly state.

If such is the case, then, whatever God may be to us, He is not our *rest*. A religion in which God is not the rest of the soul, in which God is not the fixed foundation of joy, the goal of hope, the prime impulse to duty, the supreme source of comfort and wisdom, is a contradiction of terms. " Religion is the maintenance of a real relation with the personal God, or with a Divine Person really incarnate in Jesus Christ. Accordingly religion, both Jewish and Christian, is described as a covenant; it is a bond or understanding between the nation or the soul and God; or, still more, it is personal communion with God. 'That which we have seen and heard,' says John, 'declare we unto you, that ye also may have communion with us; and truly our communion is with the Father and with His Son Jesus Christ.'"[1]

This is the very spirit of this verse. The Psalmist exhorts his soul to return unto its rest; not because it has heard of God, or has seen His power in nature; not because he recognizes Divine order in the universe, not because his poetical feeling is kindled by the thought of Divine majesty and glory, but because *he has had personal dealings with God.* "Return unto thy rest, O my soul, for the Lord hath *dealt* bountifully with thee." I supplicated Him, He "heard" my supplication. I was brought low, He "helped" me: He "delivered my soul from death." He wiped the tears from my eyes and gave His angels charge to keep my feet from falling. Therefore, on my side, I too, will deal with Him. I will "call" upon Him: I will "rest" in Him: I will "walk before" Him: I will "believe" in Him: I will "pay my vows" to Him.

We really need to get back to the old Hebrew conception of God's relation to man. There, everything was pushed back to rest on God. Was a man a farmer? The fruitfulness of his fields depended upon God. "*Thou* visetest the earth and waterest it. *Thou* preparest them corn when Thou hast so provided for it. *Thou* waterest the ridges thereof, abundantly: *Thou* settlest the furrows thereof. *Thou* makest it soft with showers. *Thou* crownest the year with *Thy* goodness."[2] Was he a warrior? God was the Lord of Hosts. His defence and his victory

---

[1] Liddon: "Some Elements of Religion."   [2] Psalm lxv. 9-11.

were of God. "Though an host should encamp against me, my heart shall not fear; though war should rise up against me, in this will I be confident. The LORD is my light and my salvation."[1] Was he an inquirer about his destiny? He left it in God's hand. "*Thou* wilt not leave my soul in the realm of the dead."[2] "I shall be satisfied with *Thy* likeness when I awake."[3] And everywhere where we put natural causes—wind, rain, lightning, armies, statesmanship—the Hebrew put God. He overleaped all the secondary causes, and went back to the first Cause; whereas our modern thought is prone to emphasize the secondary causes and sometimes to ignore the first Cause altogether.

I say we need to get back to this old Hebrew directness of relation between God and man. But we never can do so through any conception of God which makes Him less than a *personal* Father in Heaven. If God is merely a law, a settled order, we may as well give up all thought of finding rest in that. The moment the personal God is taken away, and an abstract law substituted, we are robbed of prayer, of worship, of spiritual communion, of heavenly love, of faith, of thanksgiving,—of the whole range of moral affections and acts which must attach to the object of the soul's rest. A law has no wisdom, no foresight, no love. You cannot pray to a law; you cannot bow at the shrine of gravitation, nor sing praises to cohesion. Not until you get a person behind the law, can you look up to the heavens for justice or mercy, or send up petitions and thanksgivings from earth.

---

[1] Psalm xxvii. 1, 3.   [2] Psalm xvi. 10.   [3] Psalm xvii. 15.

Now let us look at three questions in the light of this thought of the soul's rest, all of them practical questions which every thoughtful man asks. "Whence do I come?" "How shall my life be ordered?" "Whither am I going?" No soul is at rest until it can answer these three questions; and no soul will ever find rest until it shall have found its answer in God.

As to the first of these questions—"Whence did I come?" Modern thought is seeking rest for itself, not in God, but in scientific theories of the origin of man. We have no fault to find with such researches. They are right, they are wholesome, they widen the range of our knowledge. But after all, a human soul is not set at rest by the pursuit or by the discovery of a theory, not even if the theory should prove to be correct. A soul is a moral being, and its moral cravings are not satisfied by solving an intellectual problem; and the question of man's origin is quite as much a moral question as a question of natural philosophy. It is quite as important to you and to me to know what makes will, and conscience, and hope, and love, as to know what makes bone and muscle. It makes some difference to us as moral and intellectual beings whether we are linked to heaven or to the dust.

Well, then, suppose that in your search for a resting-point in the matter of your origin, you get back to this. You were not created by any God. A mass of pulp called protoplasm produced you by its own inherent force. Will that set you at rest? Can you, a being with reason and affections and tastes and aspirations, look back to that mass of matter, and say, "Return unto thy rest, O my soul: be content that this gave you being: you sprang from matter?" Is there a child who would not ask at once, "*Who made the matter?* Who gave it power to produce you?" Was it not the most natural of all things for the heathen, who was taught the old Indian fable that the world stood on a tortoise, and the tortoise on a serpent, to go below tortoise and serpent, and ask what was under both? So, if you are forced back to matter for your origin, you are not at rest, for you ask,—"What is behind matter?" And if you are convinced that there is nothing, I ask if that conviction is restful? No, no. You are a child, and the child's instinct is strong in you. Something deeper than reason, that something which even now, old man that you are, makes your heart swell and your eye moisten every time you look at your father's picture, sends you wandering and groping through God's universe for your Father and Creator. Rest! Your connection with heaven has been cut: your relationship with the clod has been established: you have been severed from all those moral influences which the thought of a personal Creator is adapted to produce. Of what use is it any more to tell you to remember your Creator? To what will you say, "I will praise *Thee*, for I am fearfully and wonderfully made?"[1] To that little mass of matter? Shall you be warned against defiling the temple of the body, and be told that the temple is holy because it is the temple of—*protoplasm?*

But the scientist will say, "We are seeking truth; and a thing is not necessarily true because it is restful. Truth

---

[1] Psalm cxxxix. 14.

is better than rest." I grant that. If I must choose between truth and rest, let it be truth at all hazards. I know of no one who makes a firmer stand for that principle than Christ. He will have no peace at the expense of truth: He went to the cross on that issue. All I say now is that the scientist does not give you anything restful, even if he succeeds in proving that God had no hand in your creation. You go on craving a Father in heaven just the same. You are restless as ever, no less restless than the child who knows his mother is in her grave, but who, nevertheless, cries for her unceasingly. You want the truth, but may not your filial instinct be truthful? May not your sense of sonship be a sense of a stupendous truth?

To go on now to the second great question, the conduct of life. How shall I live? How make the most and best of life? What guides shall I follow? Here again we find a point of rest only in a personal God, a God of providence, who *interferes*, (I am not afraid of the term) in our affairs. You may prove, if you can, that your life moves on under the guidance of mere, settled, mechanical order. That conclusion will not give you rest. You have met with some great misfortune, let us say. You sit down and go over the history of years in detail, and call up every event, and piece all together, and see how one joins itself to the other, and think you know how it all came about. Is there any rest in that? Suppose you *do* know just how you lost your fortune, just how you were bereaved of your children, just by what succession of causes your business was ruined:—what then? Does the wounded man smart any the less because he knows who wounded him and with what kind of a weapon it was done? Suppose you satisfy yourself that you are swept along in the orbit of natural law, with no God at the centre. Is that conclusion restful? Why there is no thought more terrible or more harrowing than that thought of material law without God. Have you ever sounded the depth of meaning that lies in Paul's words to the Ephesians, where he is describing their moral condition before they believed on Christ, and ends the description with "without God in the world?"[1] If you look at that word "world," you find that it is the word which originally meant "order;" and which the Greeks transferred to the universe as indicating its harmony and order. The succession of the words is startling; "Godless" amid the great settled order of the universe. Well might he add "having no hope." There is something awful, cruel, in the inexorableness of natural law, if one cannot discern a Father back of it. Niagara leaves on the mind an impression of terror which sometimes well nigh swallows up the sense of its beauty, because of this suggestion of pitiless, remorseless power. To stand and see that current moving straight towards the precipice, with its tremendous volume, its resistless sweep, and then to think of it as mere brute force, obeying a fixed law, no pity in that boiling flood, compelled by the very law of its being to destroy you if you fall into its grasp—that is a picture of the order of the world without God. There is no rest in such a picture. If it be all true—God forbid it should be—but if it be true that we

---

[1] Ephesians ii. 12.

are without God in the world, the orderly world of matter, which turns not one jot from its course because your heart aches, or my dearest treasures lie in its track, the materialist is welcome to all the consolation and rest he can get out of the truth. So of the world of society. If this world of men which we see and of which we are a part, with all its clashing and contradiction, its triumph of evil and its struggle of good, is uncontrolled by a Supreme Will, if men like grains of sand, merely fly before the wind that drives them against the rocks and against each other, if change, and sickness, and ruin, and death come just as the water shoots the precipice, just as two and two make four,—it is but mockery to point our souls to such a conception of life and say, "Return unto thy rest, O my soul." We can obtain a calm, restful outlook upon life, a tranquil, cheerful participation in life, only as we get back to God. We find these only when Christ leads us as he led the disciples of old to the market, and points to the little dead sparrow, and says—"Your Father marked its fall; fear not, ye are of more value than many sparrows."[1] We shall not be frightened at a mystery, provided we know God is behind it. We can sit patiently and cheerfully before closed doors if we know that God is within. We can look out tranquilly upon the confusion around us, yea, feel its terrible whirl undismayed, while we feel the Rock of Ages under our feet, and know that all things work together for good to them that love God. So we will return unto our rest. We will look out upon the graves of our dead, and assure our-

---

[1] Matthew x. 29, 31.

The Gate to Rest.   225

selves that they are not mere pitfalls into which our beloved have helplessly stumbled under a push from a blind fate, but resting-places where infinite tenderness has laid them, and where fatherly care watches over their sleep. We are sick, and we know why perhaps, but our rest is in going back to a higher " why," in knowing that there is a reason for our trial in the infinite mind, looking toward our growth in purity and in power. We will rejoice in law, but chiefly as it is the outcome of fatherhood. The statutes which delight us shall rejoice our hearts because they are the Lord's.[1]

And, once more, the soul finds no rest as regards the question of destiny, until it finds it in God. Ah, how little, comparatively, we know of the world to come, and how little rest we are likely to get by constructing or studying theories about it. Take heaven, for instance, and begin to inquire where heaven is, and what heaven is, and to what conditions it is going to introduce us, and instead of finding rest, we shall find ourselves in a mist of endless speculation, and shall come back from our researches no wiser than we went. Whatever restful thought of heaven we have, whatever knowledge of its conditions we have, comes entirely from the moral quality of heaven, and therefore from the thought of God; for, take out God from the universe, and no determinate moral quality is left anywhere, in heaven or in earth. Heaven is heaven to us because God is there; because God's law rules there absolutely; because its happiness is the happiness of perfect moral order. Take the Father out of it, and

---

[1] Psalm xix. 8.

10*

you have an eternal waste, unthrilled by a single pulsation of love or sympathy or praise. And, as respects that terrible subject of retribution, that subject which grows darker and darker the more it is studied, we shall get little rest out of theories. We shall get little satisfaction in efforts to reconcile our sympathies with our convictions of divine justice. After we shall have done our best, we shall still be burdened, and compelled to go back for rest to the simple thought of God; to go back in faith, not with knowledge, and to base our conviction of the rightness and harmony of all the developments of the coming world in every moral sphere, upon the simple truth that God doeth all things well. It was well said by a poet whom our countrymen have learned to revere : " I do believe that the Divine love and compassion follow us in all worlds, and that the Heavenly Father will do the best that is possible for every creature He has made. What that will be must be left to His infinite wisdom and goodness." [1]

That this point of rest may be clearly, sharply defined to us, God presents himself in Christ as the Soul's rest. In Christ He stands, saying to a restless world, "Come unto me all ye that labor and are heavy laden, and I will give you rest." [2] He has not meant that the soul's rest should be hidden away under figures and metaphors, withdrawn afar off in the vague splendor of the heavens. The incarnate Rest comes down to man. The God of rest becomes man, and the life and the words of the Son of Man are a thousandfold echo of the words, "Return unto thy rest, O my soul."

.[1] Whittier.   [2] Matthew xi. 28.

Jesus sets forth an economy of salvation, which points back of itself to a condition of lost sonship, and so tells us we are by creation sons of God, while it is instinct with the promise to restore us to that forfeited sonship. Are we not reminded by Him of our high lineage, as he teaches us to say "Our Father"? as he says, "He that hath seen Me hath seen the Father"? [1]

Do we ask concerning the basis, the order, the conduct of our life? Again Christ answers us, as his life reminds us of one who ever rested in God and walked with God; who, when forsaken by all, could say, "I am not alone, for the Father is with me;" [2] a life which took all its impulses from God, and the motto of which was, "My meat is to do the will of Him that sent me, and to finish His work." [3]

And as to destiny, even now the Savior's words come back to us from the upper chamber, "Until the day when I drink it new with you in My father's kingdom." [4] "In my father's house are many mansions, I go to prepare a place for you, and I will come again and receive you unto Myself, that where I am, there ye may be also." [5] He needed to say nothing more. That is Christ's description of heaven:—"Where I am;" a description which seems meagre and vague to careless thought and to shallow experience, but which grows in brightness and beauty and suggestiveness, as we penetrate deeper into the life of faith, and know more of Him whom to know aright is life eternal.

---

[1] John xiv. 9.   [3] John iv. 34.
[2] John xvi. 32.   [4] Matthew xxvi. 29.
            [5] John xiv. 23.

THE GATE TO THE HERI-
TAGE.

PSALM CXIX.

(111) "Thy testimonies have I taken as an heritage forever;
For they are the rejoicing of my heart."

XIV.

THE GATE TO THE HERITAGE.

A HERITAGE is something which appeals to every man. There never yet was a man who was not deeply interested in the reading of his father's will. There never was a son who did not walk over his father's estate with the thought —these acres will one day be mine.

Thus, by establishing a parallel between an earthly and a heavenly heritage, Inspiration seeks to draw the thought from the material to the spiritual; to set it instituting comparisons, and thus to bring home to it the transcendent superiority of the divine heritage over the world's lands and gold.

A testimony is a *witness*. By the testimonies of God we mean, all those things by which He bears witness to His own character and perfections. Thus His testimonies include the evidences of His wisdom and power and love in nature; the traces of His purpose and work in human history, and His express declarations concerning Himself in His written Word.

This vast and various range of testimonies is the heritage of His children.

An inheritance carries with it two sets of suggestions: the one having reference to the past, and the other to the future. We will take these two classes of suggestions, and try to find their parallels in the heritage of God's testimonies.

First then, an inheritance suggests the past. The heir, as he looks at the bundles of deeds and certificates, as he inspects the various tenements, and walks abroad over the acres of pasture and forest, or examines the vast mining or manufacturing establishments, sees in these the results of a long and laborious past. These things did not come into his parent's hand in a night. They represent careful planning, slow and gradual accumulation, widening of experience, growth of power. They represent toil and conflict and suffering. They tell too of forecast, which, far back in the years before the heir was born, was planning and working towards the rich result which is now his own. With this, too, come tenderer and nobler thoughts. There is a sense of honest pride in the inheritance, as it bears the mark of character, of the father's energy, integrity, wisdom, love for his children, and noble uses of power. Death sets its seal upon all, and makes even the most common material thing an awakener of the love which lies buried in a father's tomb.

In like manner the testimonies of God point us back of themselves. A mountain with its crags and peaks and forests may be a picturesque object to the eye, or a good stand-point for an outlook: but it will have a far deeper interest for us if we know with what throes the strata piled themselves up, what powers of the air cut the peaks into those fantastic shapes, if we can read the stories of earthquake and fire and deluge and iceberg written upon those rocks. So, it is not enough that we *receive* and *enjoy* the testimonies of God. We do not truly inherit them if we fail to *study* them. Their value to us lies largely in their history.

We shall, perhaps, deal with the subject more easily, if we confine ourselves to God's testimonies as represented by the Bible. For, while it is true that these testimonies are to be found both in nature and in the whole history of humanity, yet it is also true that the Bible gathers into itself and represents all these classes of testimony, and, what is most important, interprets them in the common light of one ruling idea—the saving purpose of God. A great deal of discussion, and a great many charges of bigotry and narrowness might be saved if it were clearly appreciated that the Bible is God's testimony, not because it contains the only testimony to God, but because it is *the key to all testimony* from whatever quarter. A great mass of the heritage of God's testimony lies outside of Bible times and in regions not distinctively religious : but the Bible alone teaches us how to read this testimony, or rather teaches us the great principle on which it should be read. It is the schedule according to which the various items of the heritage are to be classed : and Bible history is valuable, therefore, not because it is the only significant history in respect of morals and religion, but because in it, we are distinctly pointed to *God's* movement ; because we are there shown a history developing along lines of providence. There, for example, is the history of Abraham. Take the naked historic facts, and the historian might say,—" it is only the record of the migration of an oriental tribe or family, of the same class with the movement of the Huns upon Western Europe, or of the Tartars upon Russia." But it is just at this point that the Bible guards us. It says that Abraham's movement means more than this. It shows us not only that Abraham had an outlook into the future, but that it was a *moral* outlook; that a divine call impelled him; and that his going out from his country and kindred was the first step of a process which culminated in the Hebrew civilization.[1] As we trace the movement through Isaac and Jacob, Joseph and Pharaoh, Moses and Egypt and the Desert and Canaan, we are never suffered to lose sight of the fact that this story is a testimony to God: to His power and love and foresight. In the *romance* of Bethel, and of the sale of Joseph, and of the hiding and finding of Moses, we are ever confronted with the *fact*,—this is God's work. Thus this testimony has a double purpose and value. It is not only the record of God's work and purpose in that particular history, but it teaches us how to look at *all* history. When you turn from your Bible to Gibbon, for instance, and begin to see the rude northern nations coming to the front, and the empire divided, and the seat of dominion shifted to the East, you are not to think that you leave God behind: you are to search equally for God's intent, and to read this history equally with the other in that light. The barbarians meant something when they moved upon Rome, but God meant something too. Thus the Bible itself, instead of narrowing our heritage of testimonies to God, teaches us how large it is.

If we sit down with the Apostle's words, "all things

---

[1] This is admirably developed in the first chapter of Mozley's "Ruling Ideas of the Early Ages."

The Gate to the Heritage. 235

are yours," [1] and begin to examine our heritage, we shall be led irresistibly back to the past. For instance, what a heritage of *years* we shall find wrapped up in that sentence; years that have yielded their rich result to the present. How slowly God has suffered our heritage of experience and tradition and example to accumulate: how prodigal He has been of time. Take the history of Israel alone. God might have called into being by a word a nation thoroughly equipped with all the conditions of civilization, but he preferred to let it grow, and it grew leisurely enough. No haste while Jacob was pining in loneliness, and Joseph rising to honor in the Egyptian court. No haste, while Moses was receiving his careful training in the Egyptian schools, and maturing in the solitudes of Horeb. No haste to tide over those weary years of Israel's wandering in the wilderness. No haste through that strange, wild period of ferment, which threw to the surface Deborah and Gideon and Sampson, when there was no king in Israel and every man did that which was right in his own eyes. No haste in the long succession of degenerate kings at Samaria and Jerusalem. No haste in the weary years beside the willows of Babylon, where, at last, Israel learned that the Lord is one God.

And, in the growth of these long, weary centuries, what a rich variety of testimonies God has accumulated. How many laws of *conduct*, for instance, have taken shape in the various situations in which the men of the Bible history have been placed; how many shining examples of

---
[1] 1 Corinthians iii. 21.

distinct virtues; patience in Job, faith in Abraham, fidelity in Moses, brave hopefulness in Caleb, zeal in Elijah, affectionateness in John, earnestness in Peter:—what wonderful varieties of character, illustrated in Sampson, Samuel, Elisha, Balaam, Isaiah, Paul: what a variety of methods of teaching; the direct communications of God to Abraham and Jacob, the symbolic lessons of the Levitical code, the burning utterances of prophecy, the inspired melody of the Psalms, the Gospel, the Epistle, the Apocalypse. And the Bible gives unity to this whole mass of testimony, ranges it all round the one thought of God, makes all its variety tell of God's teaching, God's power, God's purpose, God's love, God's hatred of sin. Thus it is summed up in the introduction to the Epistle to the Hebrews: "God, who at sundry times, and in divers manners spake unto the fathers by the prophets, hath in these last days spoken unto us by His Son." Abraham and Christ, though separated by such long time, though speaking in such diverse manners, yet speak one voice, and are parts of one heritage of testimony.

Moreover, just as the thought that a father has been accumulating property with direct reference to his children's enjoyment and comfort, lends a peculiar interest to the inheritance in their eyes, so the thought that God has, through all the past, been accumulating this mass of testimony for our use, gives a wonderful interest to the Bible. Paul brings out this thought in the tenth chapter of first Corinthians, where he touches upon certain points in the history of Israel, and sums up the whole with the words, " Now all these things happened unto them for ensamples; and they are written for our admonition upon whom the ends of the world are come :"[1] so that, in counting our heritage we must not, as some are too ready to do, cast aside the past. The old, musty parchment, which the enthusiastic young heir might be tempted to throw into the fire, may be the title deed to the best of his estate. At any rate, our heritage in God's testimonies is one, and we cannot safely divide it. Just as an old mortgage or lease may explain or confirm a later instrument, so the Old Testament is necessary to the New. God does not speak to Israel as he does to Paul, nor to Elijah as to John; but we need Moses to understand Paul, and Paul to understand Moses, and we do not truly measure Elijah, until we see him through the gospel of love as given by the fourth Evangelist. Those who, in their fancied zeal for Christ and for His gospel, cast contempt on the Old Testament, and exclude it from their closets and family altars, need to be reminded that they despise what Christ himself honored and commended. It was of these Old Testament scriptures that Jesus said "they are they which testify of me."[2]

And, once more, it is always an affecting thought to an affectionate son, that his father's estate was accumulated with toil, and self-denial and suffering. It comes almost with the power of a reproach to his sensitive heart, that he is to inherit in comfort and tranquility that which recalls so much struggle and pain and anxious thought.

And this fact attaches in a peculiar sense to God's heritage of testimony. Beyond any other book, the Bible has evolved itself out of sorrow. That is the reason why it responds to the instincts of the race as no other book

---

[1] 1 Corinthians x. 11.   [2] John v. 39.

does or can. It is the history of humanity, and of sinful humanity ; and sinful humani y must needs be sorrowful. As, when you examine that intensely brilliant light which now and then illumines sections of our streets, you find behind it nothing but a lump of common lime, played upon by a flame of different gases,—so the Bible is the record of our crude humanity passing under the various forces of God's discipline and punishment ; and for that very reason is "a lamp to our feet, and a light unto our path." [1] Jesus Himself, the focal point of the Bible, who gathers up all its scattered rays into Himself, and thus becomes the "light of the world,"—Jesus Himself was "a man of sorrows," and, in that fact, becomes His people's light and guide ; "for it became Him for whom are all things and by whom are all things, in bringing many sons unto glory, to make the captain of their salvation perfect through sufferings." [2] And Christ, in this as in other things, represents the race : and the Bible, therefore, while it brings out this fact respecting Christ, is also the expression of the same fact in the history of humanity, the fact that it makes no approach to perfection save through suffering. Take the single thought of the unity of God, so familiar to us : yet through what a long and terrible process of discipline, through what a series of disasters and punishments, that thought was finally lodged in the deepest convictions of the Jewish race. Or look at the war and blood and cruelty through which the race pushed its way up from its low, crude moral ideals to a higher plane of life. Consider the individual trials of God's repre-

---

[1] Psalm cxix. 105.   [2] Hebrews ii. 10.

sentative men. Go down the portrait gallery of God's saints from Abraham onwards, and where do you find a face that is not written over with the lines of sorrow and struggle? And when at last you stop before the Leader of "the cloud of witnesses,"[1] behold "His visage so marred more than any man, and his form more than the sons of men."[2] Or take the Bible as a book. What a fight it has had for its position. What book ever underwent such a terrible sifting? How many have gone to the stake and to the block for its sake; in how many secret corners has it been hidden from the race of persecutors, and how often read by stealth in dens and caves of the earth. What toil and study in translating and explaining it: how many risks and sacrifices of life and comfort and safety are represented in that collection of translations which may be seen at the rooms of the American Bible Society. And these things are only a part. The heritage of God's testimony in the Word is a veritable battle-ground, its greenest and most fruitful fields moistened with blood, and covering the relics of the slain.

But let us look now at this heritage as it stands related to the future. From the associations and memories of the past, the heir turns to study what capacity for development there is in the estate; to examine the investments and to see how they promise. He may be disappointed; he may find that a good part of the estate has become unproductive, and can never be made to yield what it did in his father's time, or he may find that it contains sources of wealth of which his father never dreamed.

---

[1] Hebrews xii. 1, 2.   [2] Isaiah lii. 14.

The Psalmist, in thus inspecting the heritage of God's testimonies, is evidently well satisfied with the prospect, though he takes the longest possible outlook : "Thy testimonies have I taken as an heritage FOREVER." And we may safely share his satisfaction. The man who chooses the Word of God as his moral inheritance, may do so in full confidence that it will amply meet the demands of his whole future, and of the whole future of his race.

No one can read the Bible long without seeing that it is prophetic ; not only in the sense of occasionally predicting the future, but in that its facts imply other facts to follow ; present sockets, into which future facts are to fit. Its utterances are folded in upon themselves like a flower. You see certain petals already exposed to the light ; but you see within the circle of these something more which is to unfold in its season. The whole book is full of a sense of anticipation : the foundations it lays are for a large superstructure : the plans it foreshadows require an immense future for their development. If you should come, a stranger to this city, and should be taken to the top of one of the piers of the East River bridge on a misty morning, when you could not see whether the two shores were a half mile or ten miles apart,—if you could only measure a short section of the arc formed by one of the cables, you could easily calculate the distance from shore to shore. So, if you start from the Old Testament pier of God's Word, you do not go far without perceiving that that Word has a mighty span, a reach into the infinite future. The Bible never betrays anywhere the consciousness that the remotest future will make it superfluous. It plainly asserts the contrary. "Heaven and earth shall pass away, but my words shall not pass away."[1] Whatever we may think of such claims, they are boldly preferred; and if we accept the history of the Bible we must accept its prophecy, for the history and the prophecy are inseparably intertwined. The history itself is instinct with prophecy. You cannot read Abraham's history for five minutes without perceiving that God is working through him towards a large destiny: and the fact is all the more singular as you look at the society of Abraham's time, and see that it has no outlook into the future, little idea that things will ever be different from what they are in its own day. But Abraham's vision takes in a horizon which includes all the nations of the earth. All nations are to be blessed in him, in a richer future. This thought is the main-spring of his history; and, as has been justly observed, Christ himself "has singled out this prophetic look of Abraham as something unexampled in clearness, certainty and far-reaching extent. 'Your father Abraham rejoiced to see My day; and he saw it and was glad.' "[2] Christ himself tells his disciples that His own work is only a beginning,[3] and accordingly we see that the whole New Testament history from His departure onward is a growth toward a still remoter future; and when we have come to the end of the Epistles, the Apocalypse begins to open to us, indistinctly indeed, a vision of a heavenly consummation in a community based and ordered upon the principles laid down in the Bible; the dream of a perfect civilization realized in the city of

---

[1] Matthew xxiv. 35.
[2] Mozley, "Ruling Ideas of the Early Ages." John viii. 56.
[3] John xvi. 12-14.

God coming down out of Heaven.[1] Thus the great principles of truth to which the word of God bears testimony at the beginning, are laid down with the understanding that they will equally fit into the latest, perfect order of things. The truth which is sounded at the very opening of Scripture, "God reigns," will be the central, confessed truth of the new heaven and the new earth in which shall dwell righteousness; and the righteousness toward which God appears, in the twilight of early Scripture, already lifting the race of man in all its crudeness and hardness, will be the righteousness which shall fill the redeemed universe with joy and praise.

Coming down from these broader conceptions to the individual, we find in these facts a pungent caution against the tendency to regard the Bible as an exploded and effete production. Facts show that the Bible is quite as necessary to the present age as it was to any past age. Certain human theories about it may indeed have been exploded; certain interpretations of it may quite reasonably have been left behind; but the significant fact is that in shaking itself clear from these, the Bible looms up larger than before. In clearing certain parts of the heritage of the weeds which men's bigotry or carelessness has suffered to grow there, we find how rich the soil is for nobler growths. Society, so far from finding the Bible out of sympathy with the rapid growth and enterprise and bold thinking of the present, finds that the Bible has anticipated these. The young man who goes down into life

---

[1] This whole line of thought is well worked out in Bernard's "Progress of Doctrine in the New Testament."

with his Bible in his hand and in his heart need have no fear that he will ever outgrow it. It will make itself more and more necessary to him the greater man he becomes. It will lead him into paths where it alone can guide him; it will set him asking questions which it alone can answer; it will lay upon him duties which only its inspiration will enable him to do, take him up to mountains of sacrifice where only its power will nerve him to wield the knife, and point him to a heaven of rest and purity to which it alone can show him the way.

Such then being the character of the heritage of God's testimonies, is it any wonder that this heritage inspired the Psalmist with joy, and led him to call these testimonies "the rejoicing of his heart." Nothing is more noticeable in this long Psalm than the Author's unconcealed delight in the Word of God. It comes out in such words as these, "Oh, how love I Thy law." "Thy testimonies are my delight and my counsellors." "How sweet are Thy words unto my taste." "I will delight myself in Thy commandments which I have loved." We cannot read this Psalm without being reminded of a young heir just come into his heritage, ranging over the fields and woods, constantly lighting on some new object of beauty or source of wealth, breaking out into wonder or joy as new prospects open to his eyes, or new riches or curiosities are displayed in the cabinets of his ancestral halls. This heritage of the word grows richer with time. The preacher who thinks he has exhausted a text will find another sermon in it when he goes to it again. The man who goes through his Bible for the fiftieth time, finds it richest in fresh treasures.

"We search the world for truth; we cull
The good, the pure, the beautiful,
From graven stone and written scroll,
From all old flower-fields of the soul;
And, weary seekers of the best,
We come back laden from our quest,
To find that all the sages said
Is in the book our mothers read,
And all our treasure of old thought
In His harmonious fulness wrought,
Who gathers in one sheaf complete
The scattered blades of God's sown wheat,
The common growth that maketh good
His all-embracing fatherhood." [1]

---

[1] Whittier: "Miriam."

THE GATE TO THE DRILL-GROUND.

PSALM CXIX.

(133) Establish my steps in Thy saying,
And let no iniquity have dominion over me.

XV.

THE GATE TO THE DRILL-GROUND.

The "steps" or the "walk" of a man are constantly used in Scripture to describe his ordinary deportment or his habit of life. Life demands an economy, a plan of administration. When we rise from the sphere of nature, where the seasons succeed each other in regular order, and the planets revolve in fixed orbits, and enter the sphere of human life and intelligence, we do not leave law behind us. We are still in the atmosphere of obligation All the freedom which man justly claims for himself as a rational being, so far from setting him above law, emphasizes the obligation of law. Even if he is a law unto himself, he is still the subject of order. What a modern thinker [1] has said about political liberty, holds equally true of moral liberty, that "if in one sense it is a sheer negative and a doctrine of rights, in another sense it is thoroughly positive, and a gospel of duties."

We have in this verse three aspects of this truth.

I. It recognizes and accepts the obligation of moral order. "Order my steps."

II. It fixes the legitimate source and centre of that order. "In Thy Word."

---

[1] John Morley, "Voltaire."

III. It deprecates the consequences of moral lawlessness. "The dominion of iniquity."

First, then, the Psalmist recognizes and accepts his obligation to be subject to moral order. He prays that his daily life, not only in its large outlines, but in its details, its "*steps*" may be ordered. The word "order" here combines two kindred ideas,—"regulation" and "establishment." We need a rule of life, and we need also to become established in a habit of loyalty to that rule. The prayer, "Order my steps," is, therefore, a prayer for habitual subjection to divine order. It is not a prayer for great spiritual impulses or spring-tides of emotion. It is a prayer that the life may be right, and always and persistently right.

A religion which does not regulate a man's life is no religion at all. It contradicts its own name; for, according to its derivation, religion is something which binds together God and man, and therefore puts the whole of man's life in contact with God. All talk about the delights of spiritual communion, and the cultivation of the spiritual faculties, is worse than nonsense, if the cultivation do not reach into man's daily doing. You might as well talk of the rain staying on the mountain tops. If the rain falls on the mountains, the valleys will get it in the simple order of nature. Whatever comes into men's higher life, appears in some form in their lower life. All spiritual influences, however high they are lodged, gravitate inevitably to men's ordinary level of life. "As he thinketh in his heart so is he."[1] What you are in your thoughts, your im-

---

[1] Proverbs xxiii. 7.

pulses, your highest spiritual affinities, men will find you on the plane where they commonly meet you.

To one penetrated with the teaching of the Gospel, the divorce between religion and morality appears monstrous and unnatural. Yet we are familiar with it as a fact. We know the stories of the days when men went forth from the shadow of the Church, and with the taste of the sacramental bread upon their lips, to murder and pillage. We read the caustic words of VOLTAIRE concerning the younger French clergy of his time, who rose from their shameless debaucheries and gallantries "to implore the enlightenment of the Holy Spirit, calling themselves the successors of the apostles." We see how often the weekday service of the devil is offset by the devotional activity of the Sabbath, how the spiritual coldness and loose living of nine months is merged in the revival fervors of the remaining three, how sentiment and "the enjoyment of religion," popularly so called, creeps into the room of duty, and how helps to holy living are converted into substitutes for it.

There has been no lack, in these later years, of influences claiming the highest spiritual sanction, and bearing, apparently with wonderful spiritual power, upon the region of Christian heart-experience. The Churches have been swept by revivals, a literature has arisen in the interest of spiritual holiness, and yet, it must be confessed, that even in the Church itself, the sense of obligation, of habitual fidelity, of the paramount claim of duty, has not gained ground as rapidly as we might expect.

These hard times have developed some terrible facts. The strokes of adversity have laid bare a fearful amount of moral rottenness where it was least suspected. Morning after morning we have taken up the newspapers only to be appalled by another and another fall of men whom religious principle had been thought to have placed almost beyond temptation. We have turned with sinking of heart from that ghastly heap of ruined savings-banks, insurance and trust companies, and stock corporations, steeped with the tears of beggared widows and orphans; from those detected betrayals of trust, those shameful flights, those tell-tale suicides of men whom the Church had delighted to honor, from the trifling with public funds and the repudiation of public obligations. And what is worse, behind these startling developments is a long growth of moral corruption. These things are not sudden outbreaks through the line of rectitude under the power of sudden temptation. Behind them appear whole economies of fraud, long reaches of villainy, and we shudder at the moral condition of the man who could bear to be a hypocrite so long.

Now Christianity is not a failure, nor has moral integrity departed from the Church or from the world; but these and other facts show that the religious teaching of this day cannot afford to weaken the emphasis on the connection between religion and right living. From whatever cause, there has crept into the Church a subtle sorcery which has bewitched the eyes of too many Christian men and women, and has made them see two things where they ought to see but one. Insensibly to themselves, not a few have come to look at their devotions and their spiritual exercises as practically belonging to a different order from their daily living. Religion has taken on the character of a distinct economy, into which they might pass, on occasion, from the shop or from the professional arena, as from one house to another. And these have not seen that feeling and living, religious sentiment and religious practice, their state of mind and the state of their accounts, their administration of Church charities, and their business dealing with the widow and the orphan their feelings in prayer-meeting and their tempers at home, properly belong together and ought to be of one piece.

Is the Church's teaching entirely blameless of this state of things? Has this moral order been sufficiently pressed upon each man as he came under the Church's care? Has he been made to feel that though a freeman in CHRIST JESUS, and under a new commandment, he was under a commandment still? We talk a good deal about preaching the Gospel instead of the law, but are we not in some danger of forgetting that the Gospel includes all that is vital in the law? "Do we make void the law through faith? GOD forbid. Yea, we establish the law."[1] And does the Church impress the minds of its new converts as a sphere in which their footsteps are watched over, in which they are getting ordered in GOD's Word, and being taught how to live in the world? Is it not true that, in many of our Churches, young Christians have somehow received the impression that their great work was to learn how to speak or to pray in religious meetings, or to do some work which centred in a Church association and revolved round the Church edifice or the Sunday-School room, instead of discovering that their first business was to learn

---

[1] Romans iii. 31.

how to carry Church influences into their home or school-life; how to bring these to bear in making them diligent and faithful, in controlling their tempers and in making them gentle and unselfish?

Is it not true that some Christians have lost hold of the connection between religious enjoyment and duty? There is a religious sensuousness which presents a much more subtle temptation than worldly pleasure to a certain class of minds, which practically sacrifices Christian duty to Christian joy or what passes for such, and which turns away from all that cannot feed this craving for joyful and exultant frames of mind.

For example, talk with our mission pastors, and they will tell you that not a few of their young people, professing Christians, the very ones who need to be impressed with this thought of divine order, the very ones who need systematic, careful religious training—run away from these influences and betake themselves to hall services, or to "Gospel Tents," to listen to the speaking or to sing in the choirs. And why do they go? Ask them and they will unlock the whole secret in a word. They have "*a better time,*" and religion with many of them means simply this—the having a good time. The steady influences which tend to make them thoughtful, to lead them to self-examination, to make them conscientious and intelligent in Christian service, are not as pleasing as the stir of a superficial religious sentiment created by crowds and by the contagion of popular song.

That thing is not peculiar to missions either. Take the regular Church services on Sabbath or week-day. It does sometimes seem as if the sense of duty had ceased to attach to these; as if the covenant into which a people entered with their pastor, to hold up his hands and to sustain him in the discharge of his duties, were supposed to be binding only at each one's pleasure. But the point is this, that you are very apt to find these same people at *exceptional* services—services which carry along with them a great popular enthusiasm, and under the power of which they have a good time. No one objects to the good time, no one grudges the joy of quickened feeling, but the question is how the joy matches the neglected duty and the broken covenant. And I say without hesitation, that any religious enjoyment which a Christian reaches through neglect of duty is worthy of suspicion. Those two things do not belong together. They are as opposite as Christ and Belial; and when a Christian man finds that he reconciles the two without any qualms of conscience, he had better look into the state of his conscience.

Or look at the multitude at large. We are told that the Churches should be supplemented, and perhaps some think they should be supplanted, by hall services and tent services. The Churches don't reach the masses, and the masses do go to halls. That is the argument, and it looks very plausible. That question, however, I do not propose to discuss; only there is one aspect of the matter which ought to be considered: this, namely, that hundreds of the people who frequent such services in preference to those of the Church, do so because those services lay them under no obligation. A man says, " I can go to a hall and hear the Gospel preached, and I enjoy the singing, and I like it a great deal better than going to Church." And do you know why? Because he can thus enjoy the *senti-*

ment of religion without feeling its habitual pressure of *obligation.* If he identifies himself with a Church, duty appeals to his pocket, duty levies contributions upon his time, duty imposes a little routine, duty puts him under certain standing obligations to his fellow members, and that is just what he does not want, and why he is forever venting cheap sarcasms upon the pride and exclusiveness and luxury of the Churches. He wants to be unfettered. He wants to go and come as he pleases. It is a trifling matter to put his ten or twenty-five cents into the box at the hall, and he is in no danger of being called on for Church-work. He passes unnoticed in the crowd, and enjoys his intellectual or emotional treat, and he does not care to have religion carry him any farther; and, while I make no attack on such movements, while I am grateful for whatever spiritual power they exert, yet I am bound in simple justice to ask how much the Church ought to concede to this popular demand; whether the Church which represents Christ's economy, Christ's rule and Christ's yoke, is not obligated to make some stand for the rule and the burden and the yoke, and to be cautious how she encourages the sentiment which seeks to evade them.

God forbid that I should depreciate genuine Christian emotion. God forbid I should throw into the faintest shadow the necessity of the great heart change which must precede every man's entrance into the kingdom of heaven. God forbid that I should speak slightingly of crude Christian experience, or be intolerant of its weakness and error. It is rather because of its weakness and error, and because I know that no one but Christ can deal with it at once wisely and tenderly, that I would have it come at once under the yoke, and learn that it comes into Christ's kingdom to acquire a fixed habit of doing right, and of respecting moral obligation first everywhere.

Perhaps the Church needs no less preaching about the state of the heart, but it needs more preaching going to show how spiritual conditions everywhere touch practical life. It is a very comfortable theory that evil is so mighty in human nature that a man may as well give up all idea of moral consistency, and go blundering along any way, provided he feels that he is justified by faith. That theory will not stand the test of the Gospel. I know God's law is perfect. I know men are imperfect and weak. I know they will inevitably stumble. The Lord Himself admits that in the very passage where He tells us that the steps of a good man are ordered of the Lord. But granting all that, any faith which does not issue in character, any faith which does not put a man's life on the lines of moral order, any faith which calls weakly toward practical duty, any faith which does not charge his nature with the purpose—ever renewed amid all his lapses—to have his steps ordered in God's Word, is a sham and a delusion, and will shrivel like gauze in the judgment fire. Character is what the world wants of Christian men, and not raptures. The strongest argument the Gospel can bring to bear on the world, is a man whose life is an embodiment of heavenly order, who carries the mark of his heavenly citizenship in his common intercourse as distinctly as a Frenchman or a German does the stamp of his nationality, and who moves straight out on the line of God's Word, no matter whose word lies across the track.

For, turning now to the second suggestion of the text,

we see that the Psalmist recognizes the source and centre of all moral order. God is its centre and God's Word its manual, and to God he addresses himself in prayer that he may be drawn and kept within the sphere of His heavenly order. "Wherewithal," he elsewhere asks, "shall a young man cleanse his way?" And he answers, "By taking heed thereto according to Thy Word."[1] This whole long Psalm is a series of variations on that theme—the law of God, the Word of God as the guide and inspirer of human life. And we must look at the whole Bible from this standpoint. It was not given to teach us natural science, nor philosophy, nor history, but to reveal to us divine character, to help us reproduce it in ourselves, and to inspire us with heavenly affections. Hence, the Bible is, first of all, a text-book of moral order. It has an order in itself, for instance. To the careless reader it seems like a mass of disjointed fragments; a deeper study shows the steady development of a great moral purpose pervading it from Genesis to Revelation. Those emigrations, wars, and revolutions do not tread upon each other's heels in wild confusion, however they may seem to do so. A power is behind and through them all, ranging them on the lines of a divine order, and directing them towards a divine purpose.

Then, too, the Bible is not only the history of this unfolding purpose. Along with the unfolding goes a power which is ever seeking to draw men into its track, to put them in practical sympathy and co-operation with God's order. You must have noticed how full of yearning the

---

[1] Psalm cxix. 9.

The Gate to the Drill-Ground. 257

Bible is, how it pulsates with Divine attraction, how every history and every argument and every impassioned burst of holy song, comes round in some way to man with invitation, or warning, or instruction; how its closest logic warms into appeal, and its most formal statement has a side on which it grapples with the living soul and pulls it toward the kingdom of God, the realm of His moral order.

And the Bible brings to bear upon a man a variety of influences, all tending to the ordering of his steps.

First, it CENTRES him. Whatever the Bible is, it is, first of all, a revelation of God. It keeps God before him continually. All its own movement centres in God, all its sanctions are God's. There is no detail but is referred to God. There is no escape from God. He must love God first and above all. He must obey God at all hazards. His life must take its highest inspiration from God, his trust must be in God only, he must work on God's plans and be satisfied with God's measure and quality of success. God must be all and in all, and the very keynote of his daily thought must be, "Whom have I in heaven but Thee, and there is none upon earth that I desire beside Thee."[1]

Secondly, it REGULATES him. The statutes of the Lord are right, and are meant, as some one has quaintly said, "to set us to rights." It does not make itself superfluous. It does not bring man into the sphere of God's order, and leave him there, but it leads him along in that order, ordering every step until he steps from earth to heaven. To

---

[1] Psalm lxxiii. 25.

take a single point, how strenuously it insists on the ordering of the steps. There never was a book which pressed so strongly for the right regulation of details. The Bible will not allow us to regard anything as a trifle in our moral development. No sin is to be carelessly dismissed because it is a little one. No work is to be shirked because it is small. No place is to be negligently filled because it is remote and obscure. No man is to be despised because he is insignificant. No lesson of Providence is to go unheeded because it is only a hint. No step in life is to be carelessly taken because it is but a step. No opportunity is to be discarded because it promises but a little good. With all its broad outlook, with all its generous freedom, it keeps a sharp eye upon these details, and insists that they all shall come under its divine order.

Thirdly, it RESTRAINS him. There is no order without restraint. Restraint is implied in guidance. Yonder planet which fulfils its appointed course in its orbit, and century by century traverses the same unvarying track, moves indeed under a power which propels it from the centre, but it moves also under a power which holds it to the centre. And nothing in the Bible is more striking than this union of impulse and restraint. What tremendous impulses it gives. What a wonderful inspiration it has communicated to certain men. What intense enthusiasm its principles have created in great bodies of men. What power, what directness, what concentration it has imparted to moral movements. And yet what checks it imposes. How it curbs the ill-judged zeal of the Peters, and rebukes the faithless caution of the Thomases. How it damps the conceited courage which is ready to venture into temptation, and rebukes the spirit which would make showy sacrifice stand for humble obedience. How it cools down our feverishness in our haste to be rich or great, and lays a detaining hand upon the burdens with which our ambition or our avarice would oppress our souls and divide them from God. How clearly the Psalmist recognized this restraining quality of the Word when he said, "Moreover by them is thy servant warned; keep back thy servant also from presumptuous sins." [1]

And then, fourthly, it ESTABLISHES him. The Bible brings the element of fixedness more and more into our lives. We throw away from our ideas of life and duty as we grow older, much which at one time appeared to us vital, and the Bible encourages us to throw it away; but we settle down more and more upon a few great, underlying truths— God, Christ, worship, obedience, purity, love to our neighbor: and more and more, year by year, the Bible fastens us to these, and reveals in them new power and longer reach, and greater variety of application. We become established in our convictions as we learn more of Christ —the truth. We become established in godly living as we find out for ourselves that godliness is profitable. We become established in our love for God's order, as we find, everywhere along its track, precious consolations, new hopes, substantial joys, sweet fellowships. So with these, and with its healthful and sometimes severe touch upon lax moral fibre and wavering resolution, the Bible builds up character, conveying into it more and more of the eternal stability of God's character, rooting and grounding

---

[1] Psalm xix. 11–13.

it in love, and stablishing, strengthening, settling it in faith. Some of you can look back over periods of restlessness, shifting conviction, and unsettled resolution, and you can see how, through these, you have worked your way, with the help of God and of the Word, to a point where, though you believe fewer things, you believe those few with all your heart; where you stand on certain immutable truths as on the bases of the mountains; where you never think of turning to any refuge save one in your trouble; where it has gotten to be the settled habit of your life to obey conscience, and to accept God's verdict as final; and in this blessed fixedness you can sing,

> " Now rest, my long divided heart;
>   Fixed on this blissful centre, rest;
> Nor ever from thy Lord depart,
>   With Him of every good possessed."

Having acknowledged the obligation to be under moral order, having recognized the source and centre of that order, having prayed that he might be introduced to that divine order and kept in it, the Psalmist naturally prays to be delivered from the consequence of moral lawlessness: and that consequence is expressed in a word—*subjection*. In his prayer that iniquity may not have dominion over him, he utters the truth that sin is servitude; the truth which Paul expressed in those significant words, "Know ye not that to whom ye yield yourselves servants to obey, his servants ye are to whom ye obey, whether of sin unto death or of obedience unto righteousness?"[1] That is not what men want or expect

---

[1] Romans vi. 16.

when they seek to escape God's order. They resent the attempt to order their steps, on the ground that such ordering impairs their freedom; but they find that, instead of securing freedom, they but go from one dominion to another; that, in keeping out of God's order, they fall into Satan's kingdom.

Well, then, may we join in the Psalmist's prayer, "Order my steps in Thy Word, and let not any iniquity have dominion over me." This is not a text for special emergencies, but for to-day, and for to-morrow, and for every day, with its steps which lead us, now in many paths of routine, now through darkness and now through light; for lives which are made up of multitudinous details, which are full of pettiness and of common-place. We can take down into these no better prayer than this, "Order my steps in Thy Word." Out of these things character is built. The great distinguishing stamp which is set upon our life as a whole, comes through the right ordering of these details. O, aim for this. Aim to contribute to the Church's work and to the world's welfare this high, grand gift of character. Aim to keep before that portion of society which you touch, the spectacle of a life regulated by a higher law than the world's elastic law of expediency. And that you may do this, keep your lives in contact with the Word, and feed them from its living springs. So shall every step be ordered, and men as they behold you shall say, "He walks with God."

THE GATE TO THE HIGH-
LANDS.

PSALM CXXI.

(1) I lift up mine eyes unto the mountains;
   Whence should my help come?
(2) My help (cometh) from Jehovah,
   The Maker of heaven and earth.
(3) May He not suffer thy foot to be moved;
   May He that keepeth thee not slumber.
(4) Behold, He doth neither slumber nor sleep
   That keepeth Israel.
(5) Jehovah is thy Keeper,
   Jehovah is thy shade upon thy right hand.
(6) The sun shall not smite thee by day,
   Nor the moon by night.
(7) Jehovah shall keep thee from all evil,
   He shall keep thy soul.
(8) Jehovah shall keep thy going out and thy coming in,
   From this time forth and for evermore.

XVI.

THE GATE TO THE HIGHLANDS.

THIS is one of the "Pilgrim Psalms," or "Songs of Degrees," sung by the Jews in their annual journeys or "goings up" to Jerusalem.

It has been supposed that this, the second of these songs, may have been used by the caravans, when they encamped, on the evening previous to their entering the city, in sight of the mountains which "are round about Jerusalem." Mountains naturally suggest refuge and defence. Hence it is said, "As the mountains are round about Jerusalem, so the Lord is round about His people."[1] "How say ye to my. soul, flee, as a bird, to your mountain?"[2] Nothing could be more suggestive of shelter than the position of the Holy City within its rampart of mountains; and farther, the circumstances of travellers like those pilgrims were such as to emphasize the thought of protection and shelter. By day they were exposed to the glare and stroke of the blazing Eastern sun; by night it was supposed that the rays of the bright moon had power to affect those who were exposed to them; the camp, too, might be surprised by a night attack of the plundering desert hordes. All these thoughts would blend in the pilgrims' mind with the sense of loneliness

---

[1] Psalm cxxv. 2.   [2] Psalm xi. 1.

and of absence from home, which deepened with the gathering shades of evening, and would prompt the question "Whence shall my help come?" And as the eye took in the dark mountains behind which lay the city of their love and pride, what wonder if the pilgrims should break out into song—"I will lift up mine eyes unto the mountains. Whence should my help come? My help cometh from the Lord."

There are no points in our earthly pilgrimage where the need of Divine help is not more or less remotely suggested. Experience has taught us not to hold ourselves absolutely secure, even in the most happy times and under the most prosperous circumstances. In our homes, no less than on the sea, as we walk the quiet streets, no less than when we are whirled along the railway, we are reminded of the old, somewhat doleful, but nevertheless truthful lines :—

> "Dangers stand thick through all the ground,
>   To push us to the tomb;
>   And fierce diseases wait around,
>   To hurry mortals home."

And when we add to these the spiritual darkness and perplexity out of which we so often have to "stretch lame hands" towards God, the questions before which our minds sink helplessly down, the doubts which distract and torment us,—how much of our life is left in which this strain will not come appropriately to our lips—"I will lift up mine eyes unto the mountains; whence should my help come?"

It is to be noted that the expectation of the singer of

The Gate to the Highlands. 267

this Psalm is that help shall *come down to him*. He is as one who fights a battle in the plain, and who looks to see the reserves descending the mountain-side to his support. "I will *lift up* mine eyes. Whence shall help come to me?" The question, observe, is not how he shall make his way to the help; how he shall get up to the mountains: the help is to come down from the mountains: "My help cometh from the Lord."

And here we touch one of the great mistakes in both Christian teaching and Christian experience. As to Christian teaching, we too often hear about what men must do to get near to God; what steps they must mount, what methods they must use to make God's promises available; instead of having the fact emphasized that God himself, and with Him help, strength, pardon, wisdom, *all things*, come down to us, and are put freely at our disposal. We do not have first to lift ourselves to God: God comes down to us; and whatever lifting there is to be done, He does. We do not have to climb to our refuge: He compasses our path and our lying down: fortifies the places where we walk and where we rest. We do not have to march to our reserves: when we are hard beset'they pour down from the hills of God and range themselves around and beside us, as Elisha saw them from the house-top in Dothan. I remember receiving a letter from a highly-cultivated woman, not then a Christian, but profoundly and anxiously thoughtful about divine truth; and in the letter occurred these words: "How shall I get to Christ? By virtue of what I am, I feel that I can go near to human souls, and claim what belongs to me of their best spiritual possessions, because their sphere, so to speak, is mine. But with Christ the case is different. My sphere is infinitely below His. How shall I get into it that I may touch Him and draw virtue out of Him?" There is the error distinctly expressed. The thought in the writer's mind which kept her far from God, which prevented her drawing virtue *at once* from Christ, was the thought that she must get into Christ's sphere before she could avail herself of Him: whereas the truth was that Christ stood ready to save her all that trouble by coming down into her sphere and giving her what she needed. I pointed her to the tenth chapter of Romans: " The righteousness which is of faith speaketh on this wise. Say not in thine heart, who shall ascend into heaven? (that is to bring Christ down from above): or, who shall descend into the deep? (that is to bring up Christ again from the dead): but what saith it? The word is *nigh thee*, even in thy mouth and in thy heart." By virtue of what we are, we cannot get into Christ's sphere. My friend's difficulty was a real one. But Christ by virtue of what He is or becomes, can and does put Himself into our sphere. It is with us as with that poor woman who touched the hem of His garment.[1] If she had had to make her way by some long journey to the Lord, she never could have touched Him, and never could have been healed; but Jesus came where she was: He put himself, even amid all that throng, where she could reach Him, and then it was her own fault if she did not touch and be healed. We reason as if we had got to be something other or better or higher than we are before we can expect God's help: whereas the the help has already descended from the hills. God Him-

---

[1] Matthew ix. 20-22.

self comes down into the sphere of our weakness, imperfection, ignorance, spiritual obtuseness, and from that low level commences the work of lifting, enlightening and developing us. What we want is to have our eyes open so that we may see Him *here* and *now*, available to us *as we are*. Too often we are like the disciples on the way to Emmaus.[1] Christ was the one object of their desire and hope; they could talk of nothing else. They trusted that it had been He which should have redeemed Israel. Some of them had been to the tomb that morning, and had found nothing but the napkin and the linen clothes: and now, "Where is He? He is not here. He is still beyond our reach or knowledge." Ah! what a mistake. He was there all the while. He was talking with them, their hearts were burning under some strange power, the Word was nigh them in their heart and in their mouth; and by and by their eyes were opened and they knew their help had come, and that they need look into the tomb, and strain their thought into the world of spirits no more.

The Psalm gives us two assurances of God's help, namely, His power *in creation* and His power in *human history*.

We get a hint of the first of these in the words, " My help cometh from the Lord *who made heaven and earth;* HE will not suffer thy foot to be moved." This is one of those expressions which, seeming at first to be merely poetical, is seen, on closer study, to carry one of the great primary facts of God's character and administration: this, namely, that the God of creation is also the God of

---

[1] Luke xxiv. 13–34.

providence. How positively, how assuredly, how naturally, without the slightest hint that the process requires any explanation or apology, does this verse blend together God's superintendence of the vast work of creation, and His special care for one poor, helpless man, girt round by the dangers of the night in the desert. My help cometh from the CREATOR. Here, over the pilgrim's head, stretches the blue vault with its countless stars and its bright round moon. "The heavens declare the glory of God, and the firmament showeth His handiwork."[1] Here is the tabernacle for the sun : the influences of these orbs radiate forth to the very ends of the earth : a perfect order and harmony pervades them. There are the mountains, raised on their deep lying strata by almighty Power. Centuries pass over them and they are the same. "By His strength He setteth fast the mountains, being girded with power."[2] And yet I will lift up mine eyes to the hills ; my help cometh from the Lord, who made heaven and earth ; the ordering of the universe keeps Him not from ordering my steps ; if He holds the sun and the moon in their courses, He none the less gives them charge not to smite me by day or by night ; if He setteth fast the mountains, none the less will He not suffer my foot to be moved ; if He orders the succession of seasons and of day and night, none the less are my steps "ordered of the Lord."[3] The Psalm tells a different story from certain of the high priests of modern science. They tell us that some one or something made the world, or that the world somehow came to pass, and that, being wound up like

---

[1] Psalm xix. 1. [2] Psalm lxv. 6. [3] Psalm xxxvii. 23

some great machine, it pursues its course with its whole attendant train of suns and stars; and that rivers and oceans and seas, and snow and vapor and stormy wind simply follow a great mechanical law, and the poor little man must get on in the midst of this stupendous machinery as best he can. In other words, creation and providence are disjoined. Creation excludes providence. I shiver in this atmosphere. Let me rather go back to the pilgrims' tent, and sit there and see the night gather over the mountains, and feel that the God of the mountains and of the stars is my God also. Let me rather feel the facts of providential care, and daily oversight, and fatherly sympathy, emphasized by the evidences of creative power and wisdom which I see in the mountains and in the stars. This, at any rate, is the way Scripture puts the case. The whole thrust of Scripture is upon man. The whole movement of its doctrine, its history, its imagery is from God downwards to man; and the incarnation, which gathers up all Scripture into itself, which is the key to all its history and to all its symbolism, is expressly a movement out of the very heart of God, down to sick, suffering, erring, sin-stained man. The life, the words, the death of Jesus Christ are simply God's way of saying to man, "All things are yours:" and so the Hebrew pilgrim was on the right track when he combined creative power and providential care in one and the same Being; when he recognized in the God of the mountains, the Father "full of grace and truth," and saw nothing inconsistent in God's creating and ordering the heavenly host, and in God's making himself a shadow in the heat for a weary man in the desert: in God's keeping watch and ward round the circuit of the heavens, and in God's acting as sentinel of a pilgrim's tent in the wilderness.

The Psalmist draws a second assurance of Divine protection from history. Having reasoned that the God of *nature* will care for him, he now reasons that the God of *nations* will care for him. "He that keepeth Israel will neither slumber nor sleep." The Hebrew's range of history was indeed limited to the history of his own people, but the study of that record had resulted in rooting deeply in the Hebrew mind the conception of God in history. All his education had emphasized one thought, that God had chosen his race and had taken it under His especial protection. He had been taught to associate God directly and intimately with all the heroes of his nation, and with all the incidents of its history. "The God of Abraham, of Isaac and of Jacob" was a familiar formula of speech and of prayer. The migrations, the battles, the victories, the escapes of His people had been God's work. It was a grand result. It was worth a great deal of severe experience to get that thought so rooted in the mind of a whole people, that twenty centuries have not been able to dislodge it; and it is a pity that an age which writes as much history as ours does, and writes it so well, an age which studies history as much as ours does, and studies it so broadly, should nevertheless so often press history into the service of practical atheism, and leave God out of it. But the point to be particularly noted here is that the Hebrew drew from his study of history quite an opposite conclusion to that which the modern philosopher draws from the same study. For the philosopher sees the movement of history in great masses, and under great general laws, and concludes that it takes little or no account of the individual man, and that he lives his little life and is, swallowed up and whirled away with no one or nothing to look after him. And so, whatever grand and sublime conceptions of history he may get, he gets very little personal comfort out of it, very little which warms his heart. The Hebrew, on the contrary, made all history his own. The more clearly he saw God working for the race, the more clearly he saw God working for *him*. The grandeur of God's dealings with the people as a whole, the occasions on which He handled them as one man, did not at all interfere with his sense of God's hand upon him *individually*. The fact that God watched over Israel as a nation, was to him the best reason for believing that He watched over him. The fact that God was the Lord of Hosts, encouraged him to say "the Lord is *my* light and *my* salvation." [1] The God whose unslumbering eye had watched the destinies of Israel through all the changing years, was the very One whom the pilgrim could most trust to preserve his life from all evil. And the Hebrew was nearer the truth than the philosopher. He not only won comfort, but he drew it legitimately. All the past of all men is yours and mine, for the reason that God is in it: and whatever lessons of His power or mercy or forbearance, of his goodness and love, of his favor and vengeance, it contains, we may take, and he means us to take for our own individual assurance or instruction or warning.

"KEEPING" is the key-note of this Psalm; God the KEEPER. The word "keep" or "preserve" occurs six

---

[1] Psalm xxvii. 1.

times in the course of it; and from what we have read of it thus far, we might be tempted to think that the Psalmist recognized God's keeping only in special dangers, like that from sunstroke or from the midnight robber; but as we read farther that impression is removed. "The Lord shall preserve thee from *all* evil. He shall preserve *thy soul*. The Lord shall preserve *thy going out* and *thy coming in*," an expression which denotes the whole life and occupations of a man. How complete is this protection, extending to all that the man is and does. "Thee," "thy soul," "thy going out and thy coming in." How forcibly one is reminded of Paul's prayer for the Thessalonians, "I pray God your whole spirit and soul and body be preserved blameless unto the coming of our Lord Jesus Christ."[1] But while there is assurance of complete protection, there is also the significant hint of danger everywhere, calling for a constant abiding "under the shadow of the Almighty."[2] One thought which we need to encourage is that we are nowhere safe, and not a moment safe without God: and we never shall feel the full weight of that conviction until we shall have clearly perceived the meaning of the hint conveyed in the words, "The Lord shall preserve thy soul." When we are most secure from bodily harm we are sometimes in greatest danger from spiritual evil; and danger to the soul is our greatest and most imminent danger, calling for God's continuous protection. All these promises in the Psalm would be of very little account without God's promise to preserve the soul. Temptation sometimes arises out of the very cir-

---

[1] 1 Thessalonians v. 23.   [2] Psalm xci. 1.

cumstances which make us the most safe from outward danger. More men have fallen into sin through a sense of security than from a sense of impending danger. The soul is the very citadel of the life, and if God's protection do not extend to that, what is a man profited if he be ever so safe as regards the whole world? If he be cased in impenetrable armor, or shut up in an impregnable fortress, if he go down to threescore and ten without a scratch or a bruise, what does it avail if his soul is a seat of unholy passions, given over to the dominion of sin, lost to God and to good? Hence the promise of God's protection of the soul is a hint that we *need* that protection. It carries with it the exhortation, " Keep thy heart with all diligence, for out of it are the issues of life."[1]

At the same time, it is true that outward danger, by making us feel our helplessness and throwing us upon God's keeping, has a tendency to encourage that faith and prayer and watchfulness which are the indispensable conditions of both spiritual safety and spiritual tranquillity. Charles Kingsley, in a discourse on prayer,[2] speaks of the fact that prosperity, ease and safety often tend to draw men away from God. They find the world so well ordered outwardly that it seems able to go on its way without a God. " They have, themselves, so few sorrows, that they never feel that sense of helplessness, of danger, of ignorance, which has made the hearts of men in every age, yearn for an unseen helper, deliverer and teacher." And then he goes on to show that adversity and danger are wholesome, so much so that, " according to the testi-

---

[1] Proverbs iv. 23.   [2] Westminster Sermons.

mony of history, the most happy and successful communities have been those who, through perpetual danger and struggle, have learned in the depth to cry out of the depth to God ; to lift up their eyes unto the Lord, and to know that their help comes from Him." He continues, "I know a village down in the far west where the one hundred and twenty-first Psalm was a favorite and more than a favorite. Whenever it was given out in church (and the congregation used often to ask for it), all joined in singing it with an earnestness, a fervor, a passion such as I never heard elsewhere ; such as showed how intensely they felt that the Psalm was true, and true for them. Of all congregational singing I ever heard, never have I heard any so touching as those voices, when they joined in the old words they loved so well :

> " ' Sheltered beneath the Almighty wings
>   Thou shalt securely rest,
> Where neither sun nor moon shall thee
>   By day or night molest.
> At home, abroad, in peace, in war,
>   Thy God shall thee defend,
> Conduct thee through life's pilgrimage
>   Safe to thy journey's end.'

"Do you fancy these people were especially comfortable, prosperous folk, who had no sorrows and lived safe from all danger, and therefore knew that God protected them from all ill ? Nothing less. There was hardly a man who joined in that Psalm but knew that he carried his life in his hand from year to year, that any day might see him a corpse, drowned at sea. Hardly a woman who sang that Psalm but had lost a husband, a father, a brother, a kinsman, drowned at sea. A sudden shift of wind might make, as I knew it once to make, sixty widows and orphans in a single night. The fishery for the year might fail. The young men would go out on voyages, and often never come back again, dying far from home. And yet they believed that God preserved them. Surely their faith was tried if ever faith was tried. But as surely their faith failed not, for, if I may so say, they dared not let it fail. If they ceased to trust God, what had they to trust in? Without trust in God their lives would have been lives of doubt and terror, forever anxious about the morrow: or else of blind recklessness saying, 'Let us eat and drink, for to-morrow we die.' Because they kept their faith in God, their lives were, for the most part, lives of hardy and hopeful enterprise; cheerful always, in bad luck as in good; thankful when their labors were blest with success; and when calamity and failure came, saying—'I have received good from the hand of the Lord and shall I not receive evil? Though He slay me, yet will I trust in Him.'"[1]

Thus, as we gather up the lessons of the Psalm on which we have touched, we find a suggestion of our own helplessness in the words which assure us of divine protection: we have the positive assurance of that protection based upon God's power in creation, and God's wisdom and love as shown in the past experience of His people. We are made to see that as our chief danger is spiritual, so our need of protection is constant, and that none but a divine Protector can insure our safety; and that, in

---

[1] The latter part of the extract is condensed.

order to avail ourselves of this eternal safeguard, we must live within its compass, and not think that we can pass our time at our own pleasure, and in the place of our own choosing, and then claim God's protection when emergencies arise. He that dwelleth in the secret place of the Most High, and abides under the shadow of the Almighty, he only can say of the Lord—" He is my refuge and my fortress." "Because thou hast made the Most High thy habitation, there shall no evil befall thee, neither shall any plague come nigh thy dwelling. Because he hath set his love upon Me, therefore will I deliver him."[1] Thus all the pledges and assurances of the Psalm grow up in the sphere of life in God. It is a close walk with God, a life hidden in Him, which alone can interpret the sweetness of these pledges and make them fully available. And, farther, we see that for this help and keeping we need not ascend wearily into the hills of God to find Him out. The Word is *nigh* us. God is in the midst of us, adapting Himself to our low estate, coming down to the plane of our ignorance and weakness, His heart throbbing with such pity as a parent feels towards a helpless child,[2] to keep us by His mighty power from the foes which would destroy our life, and to "raise us to sit in heavenly places in Christ Jesus."[3] Oh, how rich in comfort is this thought to such as feel their spiritual danger and helplessness; who even now, it may be, are lifting up their eyes unto the hills for help. Cease considering what you can do to get up to where God is, what you can do to make yourself ready for God, but be

---

[1] Psalm xci. 2, 9, 14.   [2] Psalm ciii. 13.   [3] Ephesians ii. 6.

rather content to let God come down to you, just as you are, and do in you and for you what needs to be done. You will rise only as He shall raise you. You will tread the high hills of His peace only as he shall carry you up the steeps in His arms, even as a lost and tired lamb.

And we have need too to learn this Psalm by heart and to ponder it well, and to keep it by us for daily use in daily doing and burden-bearing. How much disquiet these times beget we all know; and it will be the easiest thing in the world for us to get ourselves into such a state of worry and uneasiness and fear, as that life shall be shorn of all its peace. Can we not get back into the atmosphere of this Psalm? Is it not possible for us to enter into the calm which encircles that pilgrim's tent, and to catch something of the old peace which filled the traveller's heart as he sat in the evening shadow, and felt the cool breath coming down from the mountains behind which lay the city of God, so that with him we may sing, " My help cometh from the Lord who made heaven and earth. He will not suffer thy foot to be moved. The Lord is thy keeper. The Lord shall preserve thy going out and thy coming in from this time forth and even forevermore"? Is it not possible, I say? Do we believe the word of the living God? Do we believe that the Spirit of God inspired this Psalm? Do we believe that God wrote it as the legitimate expression of His children's confiding faith in Him, and of their sweet rest in His power and love? Do we believe this, and do we believe that we are His children? Ah, God tries our faith by such questions as these. Whatever the measure of our faith, the promise is sure as the hills. The help is there for us if we will take it. We may have the rest. We may go in and out assured that the Lord preserves our going out and our coming in, and will do so, from this time forth. Whether our fears centre in personal or in national troubles, we may trust. God is the God of nations. He is wiser and stronger than men ; and while men plot and plan, the Keeper of Israel slumbereth not.

"Father, beneath Thy sheltering wing
 In sweet security we rest.
And fear no evil earth can bring,
 In life, in death, supremely blest.

"For life is good whose tidal flow
 The motions of Thy will obeys ;
And death is good, that makes us know
 The Love Divine that all things sways.

"And good it is to bear the cross,
 And so Thy perfect peace to win ;
And naught is ill, nor brings us loss,
 Nor works us harm, save only sin.

"Redeemed from this, we ask no more,
 But trust the love that saves, to guide.
The grace that yields so rich a store
 Will grant us all we need beside."

THE GATE TO THE HARVEST-FIELD.

PSALM CXXVI.

(1) When Jehovah brought back the returned of Zion,
 We were like unto them that dream.
(2) Then was our mouth filled with laughter,
 And our tongue with songs of joy.
(3) Then said they among the nations,
 "Jehovah hath done great things for them."
(4) (Yea) Jehovah hath done great things for us;
 (Therefore) were we glad.
(5) Bring back, O Jehovah, our captives,
 As the streams in the South.
(6) They that sow in tears
 Shall reap with songs of joy.
(7) He may go weeping as he goeth,
 Bearing (his) store of seed;
(8) He shall come, he shall come with songs of joy,
 Bearing his sheaves.

XVII.

THE GATE TO THE HARVEST-FIELD.

THERE were three things which greatly astonished the Jewish exiles on their return from Babylon. The first was the capture of the city by the Medes and Persians. The popular feeling of amazement is reflected in the vision of Isaiah portrayed in the twenty-first chapter of his prophecy. From his watch-tower he beholds the vast city of Babylon by night, its lights gleaming, and the sound of mad revelry rising from its palaces. Then succeed the apparition of armed forms stealing through the streets, followed by the cry, "Babylon is fallen, and all the graven images of her gods He hath broken under the ground." Those who intelligently read this prophecy will see with what wonder the captives of Judah saw the great empire of the East give way before the comparatively unknown tribes of Persia.

The second source of wonder was the escape of the returning exiles from the perils of the journey. This Psalm, let it be remembered, belongs to the time after the first band had returned from Babylon under the command of Zerubbabel. The journey from Babylon to Jerusalem was one which the best equipped host might not accomplish without some danger. "The prospect of crossing that vast desert which intervened between Chaldæa and Palestine, was one which filled the minds of the exiles with all manner of terrors. It seemed like a second wandering in the desert of Sinai. It was a journey of nearly four months at the slow rate at which such caravans then travelled. Unlike the wilderness of Sinai, it was diversified by no towering mountains, no delicious palm groves, no gushing springs. A hard gravel plain from the moment they left the banks of the Euphrates till they reached the northern extremity of Syria, with no solace except the occasional wells and walled stations; or, if their passage was in the spring, the natural herbage and flowers which clothed the arid soil. Ferocious herds of Bedouin robbers then as now swept the whole tract."[1]

But again, in the vision of Isaiah, we see revealed the wonder of God's love and power in safely carrying His ransomed ones through this dangerous journey. Nay, more: the exiled band is not to return in straggling meanness as a troop of broken-spirited slaves. Their homeward march is to be rather that of a royal procession. They are the people of the King of kings. A voice as of a herald goes before them, "Prepare ye the way of the Lord." Their way is His way: "Make straight the paths in the desert, gather the stones out of the way." No fear of thirst, or of hunger, or of dropping down by the way through weariness. "He shall feed His flock like a shepherd. He shall gather the lambs with His arm, and carry them in His bosom. He will open rivers in high places and fountains in the midst of the valleys. He will make the wilderness a pool of water and the dry lands springs of water." No fear of

---

[1] Stanley, Jewish Church. Vol. iii.

The Gate to the Harvest-Field.

the smiting sun in the shadeless gravel plain. He will "plant in the wilderness the cedar," He will "set in the desert the fir tree and the pine and the box tree together." No fear of the swoop of the fierce desert tribes. "The Lord God will come with a strong hand." The people is as grass that withereth before the breath of the Lord.[1]

The third thing which amazed these exiles was, that they should have been permitted to return at all. How could they dream that Cyrus, the Persian, would acknowledge the God of their fathers? Yea, that he should be called by Jehovah himself, His "shepherd,"[2] His "anointed servant," His "right hand,"[3] and that his heart should turn with pity and favor towards those thousands of captive Jews whom it would have seemed for his own interest to keep in bondage?

When, therefore, the first band of exiles, forty-two thousand in number, found themselves once more in the city of their fathers, when they recalled the former glories of Jerusalem, and caught glimpses of a possible glorious future, a restored temple and worship, a flourishing national metropolis, a reinvigorated national life, it seemed too good to be true. In the language of our Psalm they were "like them that dream." Their mouth was filled with laughter and their tongue with singing. They recognized their deliverance with all its marvels, as the work of Jehovah, and gave Him the glory, saying, "The Lord hath done great things for us whereof we are glad." Even the heathen for once refrained from scoffing. The deliverance, the return, were so wonderful, so directly in the

---

[1] Isaiah xl., xli.   [2] Isaiah xliv. 28.   [3] Isaiah xlv. 1.

face of all probability, that they were forced to acknowledge the interposition of some higher power; and they, too, took up the current saying, "Jehovah hath done great things for them."

Yet we may easily imagine that the occasion was not one of unmingled laughter or singing. They had returned to their home, it is true, but it was to find it in ruins. The streets must be cleared, the temple rebuilt, the wall restored to keep out the plundering hordes of Samaritans; years of hard toil opened before them, and for so great work their numbers seemed small. And therefore their minds turned naturally back to Babylon, where so many of their brethren still remained, and another thought arose, "Would that they were with us. How our hands would be strengthened: with how much more hope and cheer could we undertake this mighty task." And this thought now pours itself out in prayer. "Turn again our captivity; bring back, O Jehovah, our captives." And we must not fail to notice the beautiful figure in which this prayer is couched. "Bring back our captives, O Jehovah, *as the streams in the South.*" The South was the general term for that plain which stretched southward from Jerusalem to the edge of the Arabian desert. In the heats of summer it lies parched and barren, the water-courses dry, not the smallest rill trickling over the hot stones, every remnant of vegetation withered. But when the winter snows begin to dissolve upon the mountains and the spring rains to fall, soon the parched ground becomes a pool. The channels are filled, the streams, in an incredibly short time, convert the wilderness into a fruitful field. Thus the exiles pray that their brethren may return as the streams flow down to the South country in the spring. "Our land, O Lord, is barren. Jerusalem is a waste and a desolation. Our little band is but as a tiny rill in the desert, not enough to make thy heritage blossom. Turn back our captives even as the streams in the South. Flood our land with men, so shall the wilderness and the solitary places be glad, and the desert shall rejoice."

But with the prayer is joined, as there ought to be with all prayer, an expression of faith. They do not know that Jehovah will answer this particular request. He may make them wait long for the needed reinforcements, but they are sure that this painful waiting and working will have a joyful issue at last. And this thought, too, is conveyed under a beautiful figure, the lesson of which will occupy the remainder of our study upon this Psalm. "They that sow in tears shall reap in joy. He that goeth forth and weepeth, bearing precious seed, shall doubtless come again with rejoicing bringing his sheaves with him."

The weeping sower may seem to us a conception peculiar to the exaggerated style of Oriental imagery: and yet it is not so far from the literal fact as we might at first suppose, especially when we remember that the Oriental is more demonstrative in the expression of his feelings than the cooler man of the West. Many things might conspire to send the Eastern husbandman to his field in tears. Sometimes, as is well known, the supply of grain is so scanty, that to use it for sowing is almost to take the bread out of the children's mouths; and it would not be hard to imagine even a New England farmer going forth to his sowing with moistened eyes, if he knew that his seed-bag contained well nigh the last bushel of corn in the house, and that in a time of general scarcity. But apart from the literal accuracy of the figure, there would be very much to make the Eastern farmer's seed-time a time of sorrow and weariness and danger. For instance, his life would not be absolutely secure. He might have to go six or seven miles from his village to his field, and so much nearer the desert border, from which a robber band could easily make him their prey, or take his life, and carry off or scatter the precious handfuls of seed on which the life of his household depended. So it was with the servants of Job who were ploughing when the Sabæans fell upon them.[1]

But what a change reveals itself in the Psalmist's next sentence. As with the slide of a magic lantern, he puts beside this picture of the sad-faced sower another picture of the gladness of harvest. "The valleys stand thick with corn." There are no tears now, but only the shouting and the happy faces of the reapers as they gather the full ears. "They that sow in tears shall reap in joy."

It is the peculiarity of the Bible that, while all its incidents have their local coloring, and their lesson for their own time, they have no less their teaching for later times, and for quite different circumstances. No two things could be apparently farther apart than our condition to-day and that of the poor Jewish exiles just returned to their desolate city: yet this song is ours no less than theirs, and that from the fact that under its local coloring and

---

[1] Job i. 15.

imagery it carries certain universal human truths to which our own experience responds, and on which our faith and hope lay hold.

All human life as related to the larger life of eternity is a sowing-time; and largely a sowing-time of tears. Life is a season of preparatory discipline for immortality; and the experience through which this discipline is perfected is often severe.

But it is not of this that I wish to speak, so much as of the sowing and reaping within the compass of our earthly life; for it is very evident that the different parts of our life stand thus related to one another: the earlier to the later, the time of preparation to the time of fruition.

And we may lay it down as a general law that the sowing-time, whether it be in agriculture, or in learning, or in morals, or in experience, is a hard, painful, uncomfortable time; often a time of risk and danger.

For instance, take our early education. I suspect there is a good deal of mere sentiment in the wishing to be boys again, and longing for the happy school-days. No doubt there were certain elements of happiness peculiar to those days, especially our freedom from real care and responsibility, which do not enter into our present life; but the process of breaking up our boyish crudity, of taming our childish will, of pricking our conceit, was something we should not care to go through again. The restraints of school, the turning away from the long, bright summer days, from the delights of wood and stream, to the desk and the book and the slate, were not unlike sowing in tears. We found it no easy thing to learn well and thoroughly. Lessons were often hard, and teachers severe, and the open page of arithmetic or grammar was often wet with childish tears.

Or take the young man's first essay in life: his emergence from the charmed circle of college, and home, and admiring friends, upon the first square contact with men, as a man: the getting established in business or in a profession: how many the wounds to his pride: what revelations of weakness where he thought himself strongest: what a letting down of the scale at which he had rated his own talent: what struggles with established success before he reaps the fruit of patient industry and of confirmed reputation. It is the sowing-time of tears.

And no less does the truth hold in the religious life. Can the beginnings of that life be better described than as a sowing in tears? What else is the dawn of self-knowledge? What else the awakened sense of sin and of absence from God? What was it when the prodigal awoke from his mad dream of pleasure to find the roses faded and the cup drained, and nothing left but the husks and the swine? The "Father I have sinned," comes before the robe and the ring: the "O wretched man that I am,"[1] before the "peace with God through our Lord Jesus Christ."[2]

And in this line of thought, it is interesting to remember that this very Psalm may have been more than once upon the lips of the Son of Man as He journeyed with the pilgrim bands to the Holy City. "They that sow in tears shall reap in joy." What was it but the very truth which He Himself uttered later, aye, and illustrated too, "Except a corn of wheat fall into the ground and die it abideth

---

[1] Romans vii. 24.   [2] Romans v. 1.

The Gate to the Harvest-Field. 291

alone : but if it die, it bringeth forth much fruit."[1] The process by which He reached the height to which God hath exalted Him, the harvest of love and worship and ministry which He garners daily from the world's heart and life, was the emptying Himself, and taking the form of a servant, and becoming obedient unto the death of the cross ;[2] and he who attains Christian manhood attains it in the same way. He who is chief among men, is so through service, service which has no taint of self in it : and self-forgetful service is not learned easily nor without tears. God makes us men in Christ Jesus by hard blows at self, by sorrows which cut to the quick, by losses which make us feel that nothing but God is left, which is just what He wants us to feel. It is sowing for a rich harvest, but none the less sowing in tears.

Now, in the Psalm, the two pictures of the weeping sower and of the joyful reaper are placed side by side : but in fact, as we all know, a large and thickly crowded interval lies between them : and it is in this interval that we shall find the great practical lesson for our immediate use. And the lesson is this ; simple steadfastness, patience and hopefulness all through the tearful sowing-time. That joyful harvest scene means that the sower did not let his tears blind his eyes to the duty that lay before him. It was a bitter day when he went out with the seed folded in his robe : but the furrows lay before him, and the seed must be sown, and he went faithfully over every foot of the ground, promising or unpromising, and gave and did his best. And that is the lesson, very easy to state, but

---

[1] John xii. 24.   [2] Philippians ii. 7-9.

very, very hard to practise, which you and I must carry out in our sowing-fields if we ever reap a harvest. If we can only get it rooted in our minds that the tears, and the barrenness, and the lack of promise, and the hard toil and drudgery, and the present disappointment, mean joyful reaping by and by, that these are really God's ways to a harvest, we shall have gained very much. For that is the simple truth ; but then it is a truth which becomes realized in fact only as we accept God's meaning in it, and work through the barrenness and the drudgery with God, towards the fulfilment of God's intent : only as we accept the corrective hints which our discipline gives, enter and follow out to the end each line of duty on which it puts us, not despairing of ourselves, nor of our work, nor of God and Heaven, not wasting time in tears over the hardness of the soil or the scantiness of the seed, not trying to get round our allotted experience by some by-path, but going straight through it from end to end. There are times in battle when an army cannot make a flank movement, but must pierce the centre of the enemy if it win the day : and in the battle of life there are no flank movements : the way to victory lies through the centre every time. Sorrow, discipline, hard work have got to be borne, not evaded, if Christ's soldier is ever to win promotion. Notice the way in which Paul puts that fact in those well-known words at the conclusion of the eighth chapter of Romans : " Who shall separate us from the love of Christ ? " Shall tribulation, distress, persecution, famine, nakedness, peril, sword, the being counted as sheep for the slaughter ? " Nay," he replies, " IN all these things we are more than conquerors." There is no shirking them. We take the peril and the nakedness and the famine, and in the very midst of them we conquer.

Thus, then, the final issue of these times of preparation and discipline is joy. When a life has passed through God's crucible, and the fiery blast has purged away its dross, and God's coining press has struck it, it comes forth with the image and superscription of the Great King, and passes into the world's hands as current coin of solid gold. What true man asks for any higher joy than that of enriching his race in that which makes it truly joyful?

"He that goeth forth weeping and bearing precious seed shall *doubtless* (how positive the promise is) come again with rejoicing, bringing his sheaves with him." There have been times in our own lives when we have gone forth to this sowing, hardly able to see the furrows for our tears: when we have gone up and down the field, sowing with a trembling hand, and crying and cutting ourselves with stones. It looked little like sheaves then: little like sheaves when the blight had passed over the household and withered the sweetest and best; little like joyful harvest when bread was hard to win, and financial disaster had made the heritage like the dry plains of the South, and slander was darting fiery breaths at our good name. But those sorrowful sowing days have blossomed out into power and sweetness in these later years. Did you ever go into the woods late in the autumn, on a day of howling wind and driving rain, and did you ever see a drearier spectacle or hear drearier sounds? The sough and the rush of the wind through the almost bare branches, the drip, drip, of the rain upon the masses of withered leaves, the air filled with flying leaves fluttering down into the gloom of the forest as into a grave, the delicate colors of trunk and moss all changed and stained and blended by the soaking of the rain, how hard to believe that that dreariness has any relation to the beauty of the summer forest. And yet we know that it is just that wind which is rocking the trees and howling so dismally, just that streaming rain and those rotting leaves which will help to clothe the forest trees next year with verdure, and to make the woods sing for joy and pulsate with life. So you are better and purer and stronger men and women to-day for the tears and the sighing and the desolation. You know and the world knows that your life is richer, better poised, more trustful, less selfish, more detached from the things of sense, that its whole atmosphere is somehow purer and more vitalizing.

Or take the work God gives us: in the family for example. Those children, how we cherish them! Never did sower wrap the last handful of seed more anxiously in his robe than we fold those precious ones in our heart. But O how anxious the sowing! What daily cares for their mental and moral culture! What anxious hours over their waywardness! But there is a picture in the next Psalm which may put heart into us in some hours of this tearful sowing-time: the picture of the father surrounded by his manly sons standing in the gate of the city in controversy with his adversaries, defended by their strength, and aided by their counsels. "Happy is the man that hath his quiver full of them: they shall not be ashamed, but they shall speak with the enemies in the gate." [1]

And this leads to the truth that we must learn to look

---

[1] Psalm cxxvii. 5.

The Gate to the Harvest-Field. 295

for the fulfilment of the promise of joyful reaping in other lives than our own. I mean just this; that a servant of God is to undertake his work with the clear understanding that he may not, personally, during his own life, reap the fruits of it. He must sow the seed in view of the possibility that the reapers may go to and fro over his grave to gather the harvest. And he must farther learn to rejoice in their reaping as his own : to feel that if he do not gather an ear with his own hand, he shall reap just the same in the harvest which other hands gather. The best work which is being done for the world is the work which makes the least noise. The forces which are at work to move society most profoundly and to revolutionize it most thoroughly are those of which the general public is not conscious. And the man who joins forces with that kind of sowing, need not be surprised if it be forbidden his feet to tread among the standing corn. Nevertheless he shall reap. There is a passage in the history of Isaiah[1] which always moves me deeply. God revealed Himself to him in a vision. He saw the Lord sitting upon a throne. He heard the seraphim cry " Holy, Holy, Holy is the Lord of Hosts!" He saw the posts of the door move at the voice of Him that cried, and before that glory he felt himself undone, and of unclean lips. Then God touched his lips with a coal from the altar, and purified and consecrated Him to bear His message, and then He told him that the people would not hear nor understand him. That anointed prophet, the grandest spirit that ever touched the strings of the prophetic harp, should preach to dull ears and

---

[1] Isaiah vi.

to hard hearts. None the less was he to sow: the reaping would come by and by. A long interval stretched between seed-time and harvest, filled with wasted cities, and houses without man, and desolate lands, but the word of the Lord would bear fruit in His own time in repentance and submission. Meantime the prophet was to deliver his message without what men call success. He was to draw his inspiration from God, not from success. Nay, did not a greater than Isaiah share the same lot? Who was it that said, "Ye will not come unto me that ye might have life!"[1] "How often would I have gathered you and ye would not"?[2] Was it not He who said—"Herein is that saying true, one soweth and another reapeth"?[3]

The thought of the Psalm is rich in suggestions to us. In our own life, in the condition of society, in the aspects of the times, both civil and religious, there is much that savors of the tearful sowing-time. There is but one thing for us to do; and that is to take up our seed, and in God's strength and with God's good cheer in our hearts, go forth to the sowing, be the ground good or stony, be the prospect of harvest never so remote.

The way to the harvest lies straight through the thickest of these trials and discouragements. We shall reap, only as we shall resolutely take up our lot, make the most and best of our position, squarely face our responsibilities, let the full pressure of our burdens come down on our shoulders, and work on for Christ's sake, whether men will hear or forbear. Not in spite of these, but by means of these the harvest is to come; and if we shun the weeping we shall miss the reaping.

---

[1] John v. 40.   [2] Matthew xxiii. 37.   [3] John iv. 37.

THE GATE OF THE CARAVAN;
OR, THE PILGRIM PSALMS.

XVIII.

THE GATE OF THE CARAVAN; OR, THE PILGRIM PSALMS.

THE title Pilgrim Psalms is applied to the fifteen Psalms from the one hundred and twentieth to the one hundred and thirty-fourth. This is not one of the five parts or books into which the Hebrew Psalter is divided;[1] but forms one of two groups in the fifth book (the other group being the Hallelujah Psalms), each of which seems to have been, originally, a distinct hymn book or liturgy.[2]

These fifteen Psalms are styled "Songs of Degrees:" "Songs of Ascents:" Songs of the Goings Up." The meaning of this title is a subject of much dispute, and the following are the principal views. First,—That the title is given from their peculiar rhythmical structure: a kind of step rhythm, consisting in the last clause of a verse carrying forward a thought or an expression into the next verse; where it has another turn given to it, is expanded, or receives something added to it. Take, for example, the one hundred and twenty-first Psalm. " I lift my eyes to the hills. From whence shall help come to me?" The second verse carries on the thought of *help :*—" My help

---

[1] i.-xli., xlii.-lxxii., lxxiii.-lxxxix., xc.-cvi., cvii., cl.
[2] Perowne.

comes from the Lord,—the Creator of Heaven and Earth." The third verse adds the thought of *Confirmer* and *Keeper* to that of Creator. "He will not suffer thy foot to be moved. He that keepeth thee will not slumber." Then the fifth verse carries on the thought of the Keeper and of the sleeplessness; adding the thought of the *nation's* keeper to that of the keeper of the *individual*. "Behold the Keeper of Israel sleeps not and slumbers not."

The objection to this explanation is that, while each of these Psalms has the title—"A Song of Degrees," this rhythmical structure is not common to all the Psalms; which, if the hypothesis were correct, must have been the case. It does not occur, for instance, in the one hundred and twenty-seventh, one hundred and twenty-eighth, one hundred and thirty-first, and one hundred and thirty-second. Hengstenberg says it does not occur even once *throughout*, in any one of these Psalms, and that the one hundred and twenty-first is the only one in which it is at all prominent. Moreover, we are entitled to expect that, as they have certain common characteristics, the title which they have in common should furnish the key to these, which this title does not. "The remaining peculiarities of these Psalms," as the same commentator remarks, "can by no means be considered as flowing from the one which, according to this explanation, is indicated in the title." Once more, the structure is not peculiar to these Psalms, but may be found in the twenty-ninth Psalm, in certain portions of Isaiah,[1] and in the song of Deborah.[2]

---

[1] xvii. 12; xxvi. 5.   [2] Judges v.

The second explanation is suggested in the name "step-songs." According to this, these fifteen Psalms were sung on the fifteen steps in the temple, leading from the court of the men to the court of the women. This explanation is based upon a passage of the Talmud, which, however, only *compares* the fifteen Psalms to fifteen steps, and gives elsewhere a different explanation of the title. It is due moreover to later Jewish expositors, and is fanciful, although Hengstenberg's objection that such Psalms as the one hundred and twenty-first and one hundred and twenty-second *could not* have been appropriately sung in the temple, is very far from being decisive as he says it is; since the latter, at least, might very appropriately have been sung under such circumstances.

According to the third explanation, the fifteen Psalms are songs of the going up from Babylon; that is, songs sung by the Jewish exiles on their return from the captivity. The passage relied upon for this explanation, is the ninth verse of the seventh chapter of Ezra. "For upon the first day of the first month, began he (Ezra and his company) to *go up* from Babylon." This has more in its favor than the others. The contents of most of the Psalms would adapt themselves to it; but against it is urged the use of the plural in the titles of the Psalms;—"Songs of *goings up;*"—while, on the other supposition, it would be "songs of *the going up;*" —a great national crisis being distinctly specified. Ten of the fifteen Psalms, moreover, make no allusion to the condition of captives. It is also urged in opposition that, according to this explanation, the titles of the four Psalms attributed to David, and of the one attributed to Solo-

The Gate of the Caravan. 305

and to enjoy the rest and peace of the sanctuary of God in Jerusalem, from which he should come back with "a bettered and more patient heart, to his duties and strifes."

But no such difficulty attaches to the following Psalm.[1] This is a Pilgrim Psalm on its very face.[2] It is an expression of trust in the Creator and Keeper of Israel. Its key-note is the word "keep," which is repeated six times in the last five verses. It is not hard to see how appropriate such a song would be to one who had left his home and family in the keeping of Heaven, and who was travelling to Zion, exposed to the peculiar dangers of an Eastern journey. We may picture the caravan making its evening halt within sight of the mountains, amid which Jerusalem stands. The tents are pitched, the darkness gathers, and the sense of loneliness steals over his heart as he thinks how the desert robber may break in upon his camp; and as he looks up to the mountains, and remembers how help has so often appeared on the hills, coming down to the aid of an army struggling in the plain, and thinks that that mountain rampart before him compasses the City of his God, he breaks out into the chant—"I will lift up mine eyes unto the hills. Whence should my help come?" Perhaps another voice takes up the strain and answers—"My help is from Jehovah, the Maker of Heaven and Earth." So the thought goes on. The Creator of the earth is also the Creator of Israel and her keeper. He has led the nation through all the vicissitudes of its history. He who keeps the nation will also keep the individual. Therefore he assures himself.

---

[1] cxxi.   [2] See chap. xvi. "The Gate to the Highlands."

HE verily will not suffer thy foot to swerve. HE will watch and guard thee on thy journey, and in thy nightly rest. The sun shall not strike thee in thy day's march; the moon shall not hurt thee though thou sleep in its dazzling rays; robbers, disease, whatever may threaten,—JEHOVAH shall keep thee from all evil, even inward evil, for He shall preserve thy *soul* or *thy life*, and not only now, but in all thy goings in and out forevermore.

Even more strongly is the pilgrim mark upon the following Psalm.[1] The time of the feast draws near, and friends and neighbors come, inviting him to join them in their visit to Jerusalem. He was glad when they said unto him—"Let us go into the house of Jehovah." Now the scene shifts suddenly to the Holy City itself. Our feet have stood (perhaps a strict perfect,—have stood and are still standing) within thy gates, O Jerusalem :—Jerusalem that art built again ;—thou that wast laid low, and thy holy and beautiful house burned with fire,—thou art builded again : the gaps and waste places and heaps of ruins are gone : thou art a city "compact together." Here are expressed the pride and the thankfulness of an exile who finds the city of his love and honor restored. Others, however, explain the "compact" by the conformation of the site of the city. The hill of Zion was cut off by ravines from the rocky plateau of which it forms a part, and could not overleap the valleys of Kidron nor of Hinnom. Hence the city was built closely together; every foot of ground was occupied.

Under the power of emotions excited by a great historic

---

[1] cxxii.

centre, the mind naturally runs back into the past, and recalls the incidents of the history. So is it with our pilgrim. He is doing to day what his fathers did. To this city the tribes were wont to go up of old according to God's statute, and as a testimony of their covenant relation to Him :—to this city,—the centre not only of worship, but of civil authority; where thrones had long been set up for David and for his descendants. What more natural than that, from a review of the past, the thought should turn to prayer for the future prosperity of the Holy City and temple; invoking peace upon the city of peace? " Peace be within thy walls : prosperity within thy palaces : not only on my own behalf, but for the sake of my brethren and friends, I repeat it,—Peace be upon thee."

This is one of the Psalms which are ascribed to David; but it contains some things which it is not easy to explain on this supposition. The expression "thrones of the house of David," pointing to a long-established dynasty, would not be a natural one upon David's lips : and when we remember that Jerusalem was first wrested from the Jebusites by David, it would seem unlikely that he should speak of it as the place in which, for generations past, the Hebrew tribes had come up before Jehovah.

The one hundred and twenty-third Psalm has been called the "*oculus sperans*" ;[1]—the song of one whose eye is lifted with hope to God. Whether it was originally the plaint of an exile looking for deliverance from captivity, or of one who, after the return, was feeling the contempt and scorn of the Samaritans, it would be

---

[1] Eye of hope.

often sung by the pilgrims of later date, as recalling the conditions of that sorrowful time, and as being, no less to them than to their oppressed and suffering ancestors, an appropriate expression both of hope and of desire. " Our eyes wait on Thee to whom our fathers looked. We watch the intimations of Thy will, as the slave watches the master's hand. We supplicate Thee in our own sorrows." It is easy to conceive how appropriate this Psalm might be to pilgrims in the days of the Roman occupation of Jerusalem. To borrow Mr. Cox's words,—" As the caravan advanced from range to range, from city to city, and they saw new proofs that the enemy was in the land, and the alien ruled over them ; as they watched the Roman cohort winding along the road, or saw the Roman guard lounging in the city gate, or were plundered by the Publicans who searched their baggage, and demanded the Roman dues and tolls, and felt how impossible it was for them to resist a power so mighty, and so ubiquitous,—if the fiercer spirits among them were roused to a stern and fiery resentment, those of a gentler mould might well sigh out their grief and hope in the verses of our Psalm." Nay, who knows if the words may not, as has been suggested by the same author, have been more than once upon the lips of Him who was "despised and rejected of men, oppressed and afflicted" and esteemed " smitten of God " ? [1] Who knows but He who cried, " Father, save me from this hour,"[2] may have given voice to kindred yearnings in the words—" Unto Thee do I lift up mine eyes, O Thou that art throned in the Heavens " ?

---

[1] Isaiah liii. 3, 4.   [2] John xii. 27.

The Gate of the Caravan. 311

hundred and thirty-second falls naturally into the group of pilgrim Psalms.

2.—There are pilgrim Psalms of DOCTRINE AND SPIRITUAL EXPERIENCE. Such are the one hundred and thirtieth and one hundred and thirty-first. The former— the "*de profundis*"—is a cry to God for forgiveness, a pleading of trust and of long waiting, an exhortation to Israel likewise to hope and to wait. This is a theological Psalm. Luther called it one of the Pauline Psalms, because he said it taught the forgiveness of sins without the law and without works. It reveals the two great roots of Christian theology,—sin and forgiveness. What a light is thrown upon the human heart by the words—"If Thou, Lord, shouldst mark iniquities, O Lord, who shall stand?" What a glimpse into the redemptive work of God is opened by the succeeding verse;—"There is forgiveness with Thee that Thou mayst be feared." What a testimony is borne throughout the Psalm, by the union of personal experience with dogma, that a true theology is bound up with experience and elaborated in living.

So the one hundred and thirty-first is a song of humility, celebrating the blessedness of him who is of a meek and lowly spirit, as becomes a forgiven soul;—the "heart not haughty nor the eyes lifted up, quiet as a weaned child." Would not such Psalms as these suggest themselves to one whose eyes were turned toward the sanctuary of the living God, and who was looking forward to appearing there with offerings for sin, with humble confession and with prayer?

3.—We have Psalms inspired by DOMESTIC AND CIVIC

LIFE. In the one hundred and twenty-seventh and one-hundred and twenty-eighth, we see how home and city are kept by God alone. God is the safeguard of the commonwealth to whose metropolis the pilgrim is journeying, and of the far off home with wife and children, which he is leaving behind. "Mild and bright pictures," says Isaac Taylor,[1] "humanizing in the best sense: they retain certain elements of Paradise, and yet more, the elements of the patriarchal era, with the addition of that patriotism and of that concentration in which the patriarchal life was wanting." In these modern days, when fashion is striking at the dignity and the privilege of motherhood, stamping it as a bar to selfish pleasure, or branding its work as tame and commonplace beside the so-called missions of unsexed women, the old Hebrew conception of the household, with its sense of the honor of parentage and of the sorrow of barrenness, is like a breath from the mountains in a land of miasma and fever. Would that in every newly-founded household there might be hung the twin pictures in these two Psalms—the stalwart sons in the gate, the pride of their father, supporting his dignity and sharing his counsels, and the cloistered court, fit type, with its clustering vines and thrifty olives, of the wife and children on the "inner sides of the house;"—and, spanning both, the words of the FATHER of "the whole family in heaven and earth,"[2]—"Behold that THUS shall the man be BLESSED that feareth the Lord."

We might perhaps group with these the one hundred and thirty-third, the old lesson of brotherly love so power-

---

[1] Spirit of the Hebrew Poetry.   [2] Ephesians iii, 15.

fully suggested by the sight of Zion. Psalm and Gospel answer to each other. While we listen to Christ, saying, "This is my commandment, that ye love one another,"[1] we go back to the pilgrim Psalm to see the same lesson in picture, as the fragrant oil drops from the head of God's priest: to learn that only he who loves is God's anointed, and that love, like the dew which bathes alike the lofty Hermon and the lower Zion, alone unites the lofty and the lowly,—all social grades and varieties of culture and of fortune, in the Lord's blessing of life forevermore.

The closing Psalm, if it were not purposely placed at the head of the series, nevertheless admirably serves the purpose of a final blessing. Its thought seems to be couched in the imagery of the night-watch of the temple. Some suppose that the greeting in the first and second verses was addressed to the guard going off duty by those who came to relieve them; who, in turn, received the answer in the third verse. Others, that the greeting was interchanged between two companies of the night-watch, when they met in making their rounds through the temple. Others again that the first two verses are addressed by the congregation to the priests and Levites who had charge of the night service, and that the third verse is an answer of blessing from them to the congregation gathered on the temple mount. Mr. Cox adopts a variation of this latter view, and draws a graphic picture of a caravan of pilgrims starting on their return before daybreak. Looking up to the temple mount, and seeing the moving torches in the

---

[1] John xv. 12.

hands of the priestly watchmen, they lift up their voices to the temple guard and cry—

> "Behold, bless ye the Lord, all ye servants of the Lord,
> Who stand in the house of the Lord by night.
> Lift up your hands toward the sanctuary,
> And bless ye the Lord."

And the priests, hearing the salutation, respond,

> "The Lord bless thee out of Zion.
> The Maker of Heaven and Earth."

It is not strange that Bible students love these pilgrim songs. They attach their great theological and moral utterances to the mind through simple and graphic picture-lessons. There is one word which of itself gives them a lasting hold upon the thought and feeling of all Christian ages, and which gathers all their truths and illustrations into one sheaf. The emotion which shook the Hebrew's heart whenever JERUSALEM was named, pervades them all. Each pilgrim has his eye upon Moriah while he sings, as the Moslem turns to Mecca in his prayer. Jerusalem! The glory of Solomon, the loved goal of generations of pilgrims, the bitter memory of the exile by the Euphrates, the sorrow of Jesus, the inspiration of Maccabæus, the fiery text of Peter the Hermit, the battle-cry of Godfrey and of Tancred—pervaded, even in eclipse, with that subtle attraction which drew two centuries against its walls in successive billows of blood, burden of mediæval hymns, touched with the glow of Dante's verse and moving Tasso to immortal song, God's own type of eternal rest, of a perfect society, and of a pure church,—so has the name passed into Christian thought and Christian song, that he who thinks of Heaven has always the yearning of Bernard's hymn in his heart, if not its words upon his lips :

> " Jerusalem the glorious !
>   The glory of the elect.
>   O dear and future vision
>   That eager hearts expect !
>   Ev'n now by faith I see thee,
>   Ev'n here thy walls discern ;
>   To thee my thoughts are kindled,
>   And strive, and pant, and yearn."

They are no less sermons for being poems. Their lessons are human, not local, fitting as aptly into the nineteenth century as into their own era; as fresh and as wholesome to-day as when the Hebrew pilgrim beguiled with their melody his way through the desert, or chanted them in the streets of his beloved city : and as the shadows lengthen and the degrees grow fewer by which we mount to the Jerusalem above, these pilgrim songs will be oftener on our lips, till we exiles tread the streets where they sing a new song, and need no more the shade at noon and the watch by night.

THE END.

www.ingramcontent.com/pod-product-compliance
Lightning Source LLC
Chambersburg PA
CBHW030735230426
43667CB00007B/724